H. E. JACOB

The World of Emma Lazarus

SCHOCKEN BOOKS/NEW YORK

Copyright 1949 by Schocken Books Inc.,
342 Madison Ave., New York 17, New York

Printing Statement:

Due to the very old age and scarcity of this book, many of the pages may be hard to read due to the blurring of the original text, possible missing pages, missing text and other issues beyond our control.

Because this is such an important and rare work, we believe it is best to reproduce this book regardless of its original condition.

Thank you for your understanding.

ENGRAVING BY JOHNSON

EMMA LAZARUS (ca. 1883)

CONTENTS

BOOK ONE: The "Father's Girl"   13

BOOK TWO: The Great Vocation   75

BOOK THREE: Little Time Was Left   159

SOURCES AND ACKNOWLEDGMENTS   215

INDEX   219

ILLUSTRATIONS

Emma Lazarus (ca. 1883)   FRONTISPIECE

Emma Lazarus (ca. 1879)   FACING 104

A Sample of E. L.'s Handwriting   FACING 178

EMMA LAZARUS

Born July 22, 1849

Died November 19, 1887

BOOK ONE: THE "FATHER'S GIRL"

Late-born and woman-souled I dare not hope

1

ONE BRIGHT DAY in the early spring of 1856 a band of children were rampaging along, in the section of Manhattan bordering Union Square, and the noise of their shoes rang through the streets of low, quiet houses. They were school children; their schoolbags dangled partly open in their hands and their sponges bounded up and down against their little slates. Some of them were munching apples, but in spite of this they accomplished the remarkable feat of shouting at the top of their voices without choking.

The first-floor window of one of the elegant houses near Union Square had its curtain thrust aside. A pale, small face looked down for just a moment; then the curtain fell back into place. The footsteps of the children faded away—and Emma was once more alone in her room with her notebook for her only company.

Could this girl of seven know that her parents were harming her with the love they bore her? It is true that the doctors, not the parents, had decided the year before that Emma was too frail to go to public school. They had measured her body with great care and had found her shoulders too narrow. And wasn't it true that Emma had had a severer case of the measles than most children? It did not occur to the doctors that there might be a connection between Emma's frailty and the fact that the Lazarus family never under any circumstances took walks—and that their picnics in the country were such rare and formidable occasions that they were remembered for years afterward with amazement. Sports and fresh air had not yet been discovered, not in the year 1856.

Sarah, Mary and Josephine, Emma's older sisters, also had private teachers. Private tutors were not uncommon. Nevertheless, the fact that his Emma was to be educated at home was a source of mysterious gratification to her father. She, not the elder daughters, was the favorite, and remained so even after the birth of her two younger sisters, Agnes and Annie. He would secure the best tutors for her—after all, the cost was no consideration to him—and he himself would teach her to read and write. For he thought of Emma as somehow too good for this world. This was curious, for Moses Lazarus himself was no misanthrope and not at all a dreamer. He was a man of his day, an American who had vigorously participated in the developments of the past forty years, who had his opinions on Andrew Jackson's nationalism, the expansion of the country to the west and south, and the war with Mexico. He did not doubt that political and economic conquest of new territories was the proper course for America. Moses Lazarus, generally considered a banker because of his many dealings with banks, was in fact an industrialist; and he knew that industry and technology must inevitably form the backbone of America. He was thoroughly immersed in the current of events and supported statesmen who stood for the Union and its might.

What would such a man have said if someone had demonstrated that his obscure satisfaction in keeping Emma out of the community of school life was an essentially un-American trait in him? That it was something tribal, something rooted in another era, something related to the Oriental's desire to keep his wife shut up in the house? He would probably have laughed at such a charge and have pointed out how modern he was in temperament because—as the phrase so amusingly put it—he was "involved in so many activities." Was he not founder of the Knickerbocker Club? Didn't he conscientiously attend all society affairs? Did he not hold open house for his many business friends who belonged to all religions?

It was, to be sure, a Jewish house. The Lazarus and Nathan families (Emma's mother was a Nathan) considered themselves members of the "Jewish nobility," that group of families which had come from Southern Europe long ago and were now old inhabitants of America. There was a gulf between these families with their rich synagogue in Crosby Street and the poorer Jews of Elm Street who had come over from Germany only a few decades ago. The Sabbath, of course, was the Sabbath everywhere, in the house of Lazarus as well, and at Passover, Eliezer Frank, the son of the family, asked the Four Questions as prescribed by the Haggadah. But these things were merely brief moments of Judaism in the span of Moses Lazarus' American day. Except for having his daughters tutored at home, he would scarcely have acknowledged that there were any differences between his family pattern and that of any of his fellow citizens.

Emma's first contact with the outside world did not take place through school or street, but within the house and through the magic of words. We may imagine her sitting in the kitchen, her doll in her arms, and listening to a conversation between the chambermaid and the cook. The cook, speaking of the Indians, the Redskins, says they are the only real Americans. All the whites, she adds, have come from somewhere at one time or another: most of them from

England, but a great many from Ireland, Germany or Sweden. Next morning at breakfast Emma asks her father where *she* has come from, and she importantly recites the names of the countries she has heard. Her father is distracted; he is busy reading an article by Horace Greeley in the *New York Herald*. "From Portugal," he says briefly.

Portugal! One more name, and to Emma there is something intoxicating about it. She goes into her father's study, climbs up on a chair and after a long search finds Portugal on the globe. In the evening she begs her father to tell her a story about Portugal. What is it like there?

Moses Lazarus cannot say, for he was never there. Nor were his father and grandfather before him. In fact he must reckon back a good three hundred years and more to imagine how the Lazarus family lived in Portugal. But why are they no longer in Portugal, Emma asks, her eyes alight with eagerness to know. Because—but such matters are perhaps better kept from children—because they were not wanted there. They were persecuted, Moses Lazarus answers hesitantly.

"Why per-persecuted?"

"Because they were Jews."

"What does it mean, persecuted?"

And her father must explain it to her.

Naturally, Emma had long known that her family were Jews. Probably she was aware that in the chambermaid's and the cook's house there was no Seder table. But being a Jew was for Emma on the same level as the fact that an apple was an apple, a moiré dress a moiré dress. It was a trait rather than a peculiarity. In any case, she could not realize that people ever could have been persecuted because of this trait.

2

Visitors came and the matter was swiftly forgotten. What Emma did not forget, however, was the lovely, mysterious word "Portugal." Around this word she wove dreams. Whether it came to her out of books or trickled into her consciousness through intuition, she somehow knew that Portugal was a land of mules and great vineyards, of olive groves and castles, and she felt that it would undoubtedly be a lovelier place to live than her own home. Her father had a "universal history" which recounted the story of the Iberian peninsula. Breathlessly, the eight-year-old read about it. Most of it she did not understand, but she grasped the color and fragrance of objects and events. She passed over the autos-da-fé of the Inquisition, the cries of the tortured, the killings of Jews and Moors—probably her book did not deal extensively with these matters in any case—but she participated with her whole soul in the wonderful age of chivalry and the era of discovery. There was Henry the Navigator, Prince of Portugal. There were Jews too in his "council of geographers." But that did not matter to Emma. Only Portugal itself counted; there lay her lovely dreamland. And near the volumes of the universal history stood the collected works of Walter Scott. She read Scott, read every line of him, identified herself with heroes and liege ladies, with vassal's fealty, monks and all the romantic magic of occidental Christianity.

That was her greatest childhood experience. Her dolls bore names taken from the courts of King Arthur and King Alfred. Her own name seemed horrible to her. If only she were named Josephine, like her sister. She had been told this name "meant" Empress of the French. But Emma? Not until much later did she learn that her prosaic name had been borne by one of Jane Austen's heroines—and also by Lord Nelson's mistress, Lady Hamilton. For the present Emma could not understand how it was possible to be happy when one had a name less poetic than Guinevere or, if one were a man, Ethelbert.

She did not know of a world outside the doors of her family home until, one evening when they were all in their dining room, which was hung with gleaming damask, a visitor came, a woman who was weeping. She was the wife of one of Moses Lazarus' clerks who had been killed in a street accident. Emma's father and mother looked very sad and gave the weeping woman money.

"Why did you give her money?" Emma asked later in astonishment.

"Because she is poor."

"What is being poor?"

That was hard to explain.

"Are we poor?"

"Not exactly," her mother said, flushing.

"You see, we're very rich!" the chambermaid, who had overheard the conversation, said later. She spoke to Emma in the nursery, and Josephine also heard her. Josephine was not excited by it; she must have known about such distinctions. But Emma was oddly moved by this new trait, or rather this new word. Next time the family sat down together at table she could not refrain from asking her father, "Why are we rich?"

Today Moses Lazarus was not distracted. He felt composed, in good humor, in a mood for storytelling and instruction. He pointed his beringed finger at the silver bowl on the table and said to his children: "It is to sugar we owe it."

How could anyone get rich from sugar? Sugar made things taste sweet, but how could it make money? And yet it did, Moses Lazarus explained; for a complex life, a life of work, lay behind sugar before it found its way into the silver bowl. And on its way from the fields to the bowl it really did produce money incessantly.

A father could not very well make a nine-year-old child understand so complicated a process. But he could tell her the story of sugar, a story Moses Lazarus knew very well because—as it happened—he was deeply interested in this particular segment of history.

Once upon a time, then, people had not had any sugar at all. In those days they sweetened everything with honey. Then a man came to Alexander the Great and told him that if he conquered India he should be on the lookout for a reed that contained a sweet essence from which the natives obtain sugar. Alexander laughed at this adviser; no such thing as a sugar plant could possibly exist. But it did exist, and more than a thousand years later the plant was brought to America. There it was cultivated by the blacks, poor people who worked on plantations. Still, if they did not cultivate it they would probably have nothing at all to eat. (Moses Lazarus passed swiftly over this point.) Now this cane sugar was worth nothing as it was; it had to be refined so that it would be beautifully white and good-tasting. Then, of course, there was the matter of beet sugar, a wonderful discovery that had been made a hundred years ago in Germany. Now this beet sugar . . .

But Emma had stopped listening. A fearful insight had suddenly shaken her to the depths of her soul. If sugar actually had such a vast history, then no doubt everything had a history of its own. The milk brought to the table, the cow it was taken from, everything had an origin and a history. Mother's silk dress, the cretonne of the curtains, the silver the spoons were made of—nothing stood still, nothing stood firm. Everything was in motion, everything was rushing up out of the past ages toward this very moment and toward

Emma Lazarus, who sat, her eyes flooded with new knowledge, at her parents' table.

It was too much for her. She uttered a low cry. Her parents saw that she had a fever and put her to bed. In her dream she was the Queen of Portugal and lived in a white palace of granular marble that was really sugar.

3

Emma was eleven years old when a shot was fired "somewhere in the South." The shore batteries of Charleston had hurled against Fort Sumter a shot that was to be heard round the world. South Carolina, Charleston, Sumter—these names sprang like cries of alarm from the pages of newspapers to the tongues of the people. Emma's father, who very rarely showed excitement, threw up his arms and said all sorts of incomprehensible things, as though he or his family had experienced a stroke of great good fortune. "At last, at last, here is the war. We goaded the South into firing the first shot." Anything, he said, was better than "enduring this unbearable tension for even a month longer."

Emma had, as a matter of fact, noticed no signs at all of unbearable tension. At eleven she had only the vaguest conception of what a cannon shot was. It had something to do with fireworks, she thought. Three years ago her family had gone to a country fair; there she had seen a mortar being fired, one that had been preserved from George Washington's time. It had not gone off very smoothly; the powder had been wet and the attendants had had to send off for dry powder first. Josephine and Emma had stood too close to the mortar and the rumble of the explosion had given them headaches.

In any case, cannon shots were altogether pacific matters

and there was no reason to think of war in connection with them. There had been wars in the eighteenth century. And then the one in 1812—and recently the war with Mexico. But that one had been so far away that you probably couldn't have seen it with a spyglass. How was it possible to be suddenly in the midst of a real war? The name of President Lincoln was on everyone's lips. But who was Jefferson Davis? Who was Edward Stanton? Who was Seward? Everyone talked and everyone was fearfully excited.

Life in Emma's home changed. Peaceful uncles and harmless cousins suddenly appeared strangely disguised in blue or black dress with grave, resolute mien. These kinsfolk could hardly be soldiers, could they? But since they so often carried sabers and pistol holsters, Emma had to assume they were. How difficult it was to have to relate what she had read about wars of the past with what she now saw with her own eyes: uncles and cousins in uniform! Another of the confusions of these days was the breakdown of day and night. At night the family no longer slept regularly, for frequently cousins and uncles arrived at night, spoke loudly, ordered coffee, eggs, bread and ham, and said they had to "get going before dawn." And, standing at the bottom of the stairwell, they would embrace father and mother before leaving. Emma's father would be pale with emotion, her mother silent. Emma had been strictly forbidden to come out to the steps in her nightgown, but she did it anyway and so witnessed these scenes. There was something bad about all this uproar; she realized that because of the dirt the soldiers' boots left on the carpets. Dirt in the dining room, dirt in the library! If the war was bringing so much nastiness along with it, perhaps President Lincoln would have done better not to "goad the South into firing the first shot."

One day a particular regiment marched out of New York. The Lazarus family stood in the street, crushed by a wall of humanity. A glittering stream of rifle barrels flowed down the street, horses pranced. "Eliezer, Eliezer!" Emma's mother called suddenly, and fainted away in her father's arms. She had recognized a cousin whom she had not seen for twenty years—and perhaps she had been mistaken. In any case, father brought her home and Emma heard him assuring her that not every one of these soldiers would be killed. But after that Emma wanted to hear nothing more about the war. When on July 20, her twelfth birthday, she failed to receive some of the presents she had asked for, she blamed the war and took revenge by shutting up like a clam, something she was a master at.

English literature now became far more important to her than the outside world. Literature: the grand empire of words which, after all, contained the widest reality. Her guide to it was a teacher, an angelic young man whose name we do not know. He was blond, rosy-complexioned, very shy toward adults; when Emma's parents were present he occasionally stammered. But when he was alone with Emma in her room, the look in his pale blue eyes changed and the expression of his mouth grew firmer. He glowed with an ardent inspiration. This tutor told Emma that the English language was the greatest and the most comprehensive language in the world. There could be nothing more splendid than the English language unless it were the language of the angels—and perhaps English itself was already the angels' language. Then he read aloud Milton's *Lycidas* to the girl of twelve and explained the meaning of the verses to her. Emma perhaps did not understand a great deal, but she grasped the beauty of each word by itself.

"Doesn't it surprise you," her teacher would ask, "that

Milton speaks of 'blind mouths' in this passage? Since a mouth has no eyes, how can it be blind?"

But Emma shook her head and said firmly, "Oh, yes, a mouth can be blind."

The gentle teacher tested her still further. "Shouldn't Milton have spoken rather of dumb mouths?"

"No. If Milton says it, it is right."

There came the day when Emma was to begin reading Shakespeare with her teacher. At this point her mother intervened. For various reasons—propriety, for one—it was not right to introduce a thirteen-year-old girl to Shakespeare. Moreover, Mrs. Lazarus added, the literature lessons would have to be somewhat curtailed, for Emma was falling behind in arithmetic and natural history. And the acquiring of languages, especially French, was more important than English poetry.

This curtailment, for reasons we do not know, was a hard blow to the tutor. Probably he was a poor man and it meant his losing a good deal of money. He spoke rather bitterly to Emma about it, indicating that his ideas about a "practical education" differed from those of a rich American family. He was, of course (it is not difficult to guess), not an American at all, but an Englishman. Considerably nettled, he assured Emma that England stood on a far higher cultural level than America. To be embroiled in a civil war in the middle of the nineteenth century! Now if the United States had not broken away from the English motherland a hundred years ago, this war would probably never have taken place.

With a total lack of logic, which troubled neither him nor Emma, he spoke of English calm, of the beauty of the countryside of England, and above all of Queen Victoria. Only five years ago he had seen her in London, riding out from Buckingham Palace with four white horses and a sunshade, all in white—and he could not imagine that the arts and sciences could possibly flourish except under a monarchical system. Of course, kings could be attacked; Lord Byron had done that. But first they had to exist! And their existence could be sensed in every line of English poetry. In American poetry, on the other hand, one sensed the absence of any real authority. Of course Lincoln was a decent chap—but rulers must be chosen by the grace of God, not by the grace of the people. Had Emma never noticed that Americans had no native culture? What they had was partly English, as for instance their law, partly French, like fashion, partly German, like medicine. They could stand on their own feet only in technology and engineering. But these were relatively barbarian matters, weren't they?

So the young man made a number of confusing and rather offensive statements—and then he drifted away and out of Emma's life. But he left in her a cruel feeling of inferiority that was to last for years, a feeling of sorrow that she was not English. And while outside in the world of America fearful battles were being fought, while the nation rent itself in an incomparable struggle, while the Gettysburg Address was being delivered and General Grant at Appomattox was receiving heroic Lee's unconditional surrender, Emma remained shut within the clamshell of her own self and was scarcely aware of these things.

The world outside, the world of America, seemed incomprehensible to her at present. Only the interior world of the English language counted.

4

But this was only the appearance.

Emma was a Jewish girl, a very sensitive spirit, inclined to timidity and melancholy. She could not remain unaffected by these momentous events. As in most of the country's families, the members of the widely ramified Lazarus and Nathan families saw their personal destinies influenced by the Civil War.

Of the one hundred and fifty to two hundred thousand Jews who then lived in the United States, most of the able-bodied men were members of the opposing armies. In the Army of the Confederacy the number of Jews was considerable enough for it to be deemed impractical to grant furloughs on Rosh ha-Shanah and Yom Kippur, lest "injury to the service" result. This observation was made by the Secretary of State of the South, J. P. Benjamin, himself a Jew.

Without doubt Mason and Dixon's Line severed Jews from Jews as sharply as it divided Southern from Northern Christians. The South had its prosperous Jews who bore Spanish-Portuguese names and were themselves landowners and slaveholders. For easily understood reasons the Jews of the North supported the ideals of Lincoln. A very large number of these Jews came from Germany. They were the victims of the reaction to the Revolution of 1848, and they were as staunch republicans as their fellow German exiles. In addition, there were the Austrian and Hungarian Jews whose leaders—Dembitz, Kaufmann, Heilprin, Pinner and Dittenhoefer—upheld the cause of freedom against slavery as a matter of course.

But political concepts did not interest Emma. It scarcely mattered to her when she heard it mentioned, with clannish pride, that there were twelve Jewish generals and twenty Jewish colonels in the army. Only the human being counted for her, the human being who a few months or years ago had lived, walked, breathed, talked. . . . Emma was fifteen years old, and the very air she breathed was full of the sorrow of partings. The young men who visited her house and who had hunted clams with her on the beach at Newport (the Lazaruses were now spending their summers there)—these young men did not return. Heine had written a poem about love's sorrow on a beach:

> Das Meer erglänzte weit hinaus
> Im letzten Abendscheine.
> Wir sassen am einsamen Fischerhaus,
> Wir sassen stumm und alleine.

Perhaps one of these young men had read the poem to her—so many spoke German those days!—and perhaps he had said that he would never forget her. Her friendly, blue-gray, queerish eyes (she sometimes seemed to be looking pensively at the base of her nose), her rather boyish profile, her frail, too-narrow shoulders, and, a most charming feature, the darkish down which shadowed her upper cheek—many a young soldier carried away this portrait in his mind.

The first verses Emma wrote were devoted to some such young man whose name we do not know. But at this time she cared far more for the piano than for writing verse. For months at a time she drifted along on the sea of music like a lost soul; the music of Chopin, the Pole, and Schumann, the German, expressed a sorrowfulness and longing that, it seemed to her, could be found nowhere else but in the poems of Heine.

Then came that fearful fourteenth of April, 1865, when Emma was awakened from her dreams and thrust rudely back into reality. President Lincoln assassinated! The melancholy-faced man who had become a second father of his people had fallen. "Father" and "people" were the highest possible ideals in the mind of a growing American-Jewish girl. And so she wrote five stanzas on Lincoln's death which described the actor's deed, his flight and his repentance. As yet her gifts were unformed; these verses could not compare in stature with what others had to say about Lincoln. But there is an awkward seriousness in them and they reflect something of the tragic numbness of those days.

5

The year 1865 introduced a significant new element into Emma's family history. Moses Lazarus retired from business. We do not know why. Perhaps his affairs were going badly; the South, with its sugar plantations, had been temporarily shattered. That was not to be for long—and there were other sources of sugar available to the trade. But perhaps the father's retirement had personal motivations. Apparently, Moses Lazarus was acting as a Jew whose cultural outlook prescribed that only so much of one's life could be given to the pursuit of material wealth. Now that two-thirds of his life had gone by, he seemed to wish to dedicate the rest to the pursuit of wisdom.

All of the energy he had previously expended in the outside world he now turned inward, and the children profited by it. The members of this family which had always been closely knit grew so dependent on one another that their affection for each other looked from the outside—and especially to the non-Jewish observer—almost comical. Thus, Thomas W. Higginson, a high-ranking army officer, wrote: "Yesterday I chanced to call at the Lazarus home and found the whole family in distress. What had happened?—two daughters answered me rather tearfully: 'Father is going away.' 'But he will be back again?' I asked. 'Yes—but not before tomorrow night.'" That was how terrible even the briefest separation seemed to them.

The family could not live for a single night without the father. That was especially true for Emma. At the age of eighteen, when normally she would have fallen in love with some young man, her emotional life was fixed so firmly on her father that she became more and more what is called a "father's girl." This mild, intelligent, cultivated man cast his shadow upon her verses. There may have been traces in his nature of that jealousy which Shakespeare's Prospero exhibits in guarding his Miranda. He gave her far more than at this stage of her life she could have received from any other man. For he studied with her and she studied with him.

She needed this above all. For the die had been cast. The verses Emma was writing (those verses at which her younger sister Agnes and her brother giggled) had accumulated; they already formed a small book, and that book was going to be printed. Printed? Many problems had to be considered.

Was the book to have Emma Lazarus' own name on the title page? That would be a rarity, and not only in America. Even in Queen Victoria's realm and in the French-speaking world women who wrote were still unusual phenomena, and they preferred to hide behind men's names, as in the case of George Eliot and George Sand. The purpose of this was to shield them in their private lives; at the very least to fend off those unscrupulous ruffians who insisted that "a woman must have experienced herself everything she writes about." For if she had experienced everything herself, she was necessarily a social outcast.

Moses and Hettie Lazarus were aware of this danger, of course. But, after all, the danger did not really exist for Emma—since the book was planned for private circulation only. Therefore she could place her full name on the title page. The very presence of her innocent maiden name indicates that in taking this half-step into the outside world she was counting upon the protection of her father and her family.

In 1867 the book, entitled *Poems and Translations*, was published. It contained work that Emma had written with care and diligence between her fourteenth and seventeenth years. None of the poems is a reckless outpouring and nothing in the book bespeaks the joys of youth. Rather, there is an odd mournfulness in her verses; the book opens with an elegy upon the death of a friend and continues with a comment upon a gray lock of her mother's hair. The fundamental mood of the volume is autumnal rather than vernal. Its principal merit, however, lies not in Emma's own verses, but in the translations of poems by Victor Hugo, Schiller and Heinrich Heine. The sixteen-year-old girl proved able to encompass in her translations Victor Hugo's alternations between the classic-romantic and the poetical declamation, and Heine's ambivalence of sensuality and soulfulness.

We do not know whether Moses and Hettie Lazarus were aware that in this young author of theirs they had launched a child prodigy into the world. But whether the parents' attitude was modest or proud, the fact of Emma's astounding precocity cannot be denied. This precocity—in itself quite genuine, though marred here and there by an inevitable trace of youthful dilettantism—is one of those gifts that the Greeks accounted fearsome. For nature will not be mocked. Early maturity must be followed by periods of dullness, stagnation and even retrogression.

Emma's father, who knew so much about banking, should have realized that a child prodigy is a creature who overdraws the balance of his gifts. At the very best, the prodigy consumes his entire capital at once, without waiting to reap the interest. In the interpretive arts child prodigies are not faced by this danger. A precocious nine-year-old violinist may remain at seventy the greatest violinist of his age. But in the sphere of original creation other laws appear to operate.

In other words, Emma Lazarus' first book of verse would not count. The test would come with the second. Her first book had just been published when she met Ralph Waldo Emerson—at a gathering in the home of Samuel G. Ward in December 1866. Curiously enough, Emerson was the first man of letters she had ever met. She had so completely immersed herself in the world of books that she could scarcely think of these books as being written by living men. Schiller was dead, Byron was dead, Heine was dead. Victor Hugo (of whose poetry she had translated seventy-three pages!), though still alive, was far, far away in mythical France. How could she venture to write a letter to a god? But Emerson appeared to be a friendly, paternal gentleman, rather shy in society, who lived in Massachusetts. Why should she not venture to send her book to him at Concord?

6

As soon as she had mailed the book off to Concord she wished she might have recovered it from the post office. For of course Emerson was a god after all. Undoubtedly he had come to that evening gathering merely "disguised" as a friendly old man. And one did not send poems to a god.

But Emerson was also something else—and the image of that something appears more and more frequently in Emma Lazarus' letters and diaries. Emerson was above all a lighthouse illuminating the darkness of night with his revolving beacon. This was the feeling she had about him for years. The moving beacon of his thought, with its faculty for lighting up intangibles, had long been the greatest stimulus of her intellectual life.

Perhaps she never saw quite how apt the image was. Every lighthouse stands on the verge of chaos, by the untamed sea, to point the way for sailors. But the light it casts is cold, and because of its rotary motion it hits the searcher's eyes suddenly, only to leave him for a while in darkness.

Much about Emerson was very dark indeed. Emma still did not understand what it was. She knew nothing of his life, nothing of what it had cost him to raise himself into the lighthouse he was, to become the Emerson she saw. She had never concerned herself with his problems and never could have done so.

The child of a Jewish family characterized by a good deal of sentimentality and fear of change, she had always loved Emerson's writings because they appeared to her so free of anxiety, so unsentimental, so ethereally light. She did not know that the great Emerson came from a family of melancholics with even a streak of insanity. According to Emerson's Faustian teachings, the mind of modern man was omnipotent because it could control the atavistic revolts of the soul. The man who could hold his mind in rein could guide it through all passions and create perfect harmony between the "self" and "nature."

Yet Emerson would have had to look far for any personal tradition bearing on his doctrine of the supremacy of mind. Emerson's forebears would have looked upon such intellectual pride as equivalent to the mark of Cain, and would have branded independent thinking as sinful. Even Emerson, for all his emancipated theories, had come into the world with a shackle upon him: he was the son of a minister and was himself marked out for the ministry. Minister in due course he became, and those who heard him preach testified that he was inspired by the Word as none other. But of course he soon became involved in theological disputes. Odd as it may seem, some of those ancient disputes about the Lord's Supper (whether the bread *means* or *is* the body) may have filled him with disgust for the profession.

"A cosmopolitan of the mind cannot be a sectarian," one of his admirers said. And so Emerson left the Protestant ministry and henceforth delivered sermons only in books.

Cosmopolitan of the mind—this he certainly was. And that was an additional cause for Emma's love for him. Because he was at home nowhere, he seemed everywhere at home. He was one of the most remarkable readers who ever spent a life bent over books, and his mind was fructified by all the sciences, from botany, architecture and economics to chemistry. Sometimes Emerson spoke truths too bitter for his countrymen to accept, even though the dangerous words might first be confined to the secret pages of his diary. "The aspect this country presents is a certain maniacal activity, an immense apparatus of cunning machinery which turns out at last some Nuremberg toys. Has it generated, as great interests do, any intellectual power? One would say there is nothing colossal in the country but its geography. . . ." But what, he asks, about the moral and intellectual consequences? Emma might have realized that it is somehow characteristically American to preach the spirit to businessmen, and in this Ralph Waldo Emerson was her fellow countryman.

For of course a personality of that sort could have been only an American. The liberty and prudence with which he handled the heritage of the past and minted it into his own coin is altogether un-European. "Test everything, but keep the best." This apparently dry biblical phrase served as keynote for Emerson's studies. As the contemporary of many ages, everything bore a contemporaneous aspect for him. And yet the past to him was really no more than a groundwork for the evocation of the present, of *his* age. His disciplined imagination enabled him to relive the events of all the past as though in a vast theater. However, he relived history without experiencing the pangs of birth. Expressions like "repentance" and "suffering" do not occur in Emerson's essays. Even when in his essay, "The Tragic," he says: "He has seen but half the universe who never has been shown the house of Pain. As the salt sea covers more than two-thirds of the surface of the globe, so sorrow encroaches in man on felicity," we sense that this is purely Ciceronian rhetoric. Yet the passage indicates that he understood what his limits were: he speaks only of *being shown* the house of pain, seeing it as a visitor; he does not speak of living in it. And when he goes on to say: ". . . no theory of life can have any right which leaves out of account the values of vice, pain, disease, poverty, insecurity, disunion, fear and death. . . ."—we are forced to ask in amazement how this was ever relevant to him. He knew nothing of Dostoevsky's life in the slums among the insulted and injured, nothing of Tolstoy's struggles to live in the spirit of primitive Christianity. Instead, he sacrificed to his desire for harmony, to the classical *aequitas animi*, all the disharmonious elements that had troubled his own youth. He was so eager to prove an absolute harmony, a "kosmos" that was superhuman, that he denied everything that partook of chaos.

The light was there in abundance. For years it had dazzled Emma. Moreover, lighthouses are not the only sources of blinding light. Clever jewelers can also make a fine glitter by taking a gem out of Plato and setting it into half a golden circlet lifted from Goethe's intellectual property. And when a young girl reads in a letter to herself the seductive words: "Grief, passion, disaster are only materials of Art," then the fascination is complete. Emma could not help thinking Emerson greater than Plato or Goethe because he was more modern than they and presented a synthesis of both.

On February 24, 1868, Emerson wrote his first letter to her. It was a reply she had never dared to hope for: "I have so happy recollections of the conversation at Mr Ward's, that I am glad to have them confirmed by the possession of your book & letter." He had read her poems and had liked them, had liked them very well indeed. "The poems have important merits, & I observe that my poet gains in skill as the poems multiply, & she may at last confidently say, I have mastered the obstructions, I have learned the rules: henceforth I command the instrument, & now, every new thought & new emotion shall make the keys eloquent to my own & to every gentle ear. Few know what treasure that conquest brings,—what independence & royalty." Then came that dangerous sentence averring that the troubles of life are significant mainly in that they furnish fuel for the artist: a sentence which Flaubert might have written, but which is not thereby made any the truer.

Together with her book Emma had sent along a manuscript with new poems which Emerson, according to his own words, liked better than some of those in the book. The latter, he writes, "are too youthful & some words & some rhymes inadmissible. 'Elfrida' & 'Bertha' are carefully finished, & well told stories, but tragic & painful,—which I think a fault." So then Emerson's only serious criticism was that Emma's poetic narratives were not optimistic enough? He now confessed something he would have hardly admitted thirty years earlier: "You will count me whimsical, but I would never willingly begin a story with a sad end." But at once he seemed to recognize that this repudiation of the tragic might be misunderstood, and he wrote in between the lines that the tragic was after all difficult and might very well be too difficult for Emma at her present stage of development. And then he added his coda—oscillating between full earnest and that gentle mockery in which this great writer of letters was a master. "But you shall instantly defy me, & send me a heartbreaking tale, so rich in fancy, so noble in sentiment that I shall prefer it to all the prosperities of time. I am so glad that you have kept your word to write to so ancient a critic, that I regret the more that you should have had to wait so long for a reply. But I was absent from home when your book arrived, & only now have found & read it."

7

This was the beginning of a correspondence between an unknown girl and the most famous man of the age—a correspondence that extended over many years, although with varying degrees of intensity.

The letters from Concord were the greatest event in the life of this twenty-year-old girl. Before them, her father's influence receded into the background—although we now know in the light of modern psychology that Emerson was a "substitute" for her father and thus represented the power of the father intensified and redoubled.

His letters were a curious mixture of condescension and gentle self-deprecation. Emerson kept emphasizing that his advice was like that of a lonely, aging bachelor—though he was neither a bachelor nor lonely. Yet the memory he kept of her from his New York visit must have enchanted him; otherwise he could not have written her on April 14, 1868: "You are very kind to write again, & it is good in these cold misplaced days to see your letters on my old desk. I shall not lose my faith in the return of spring. It is the more kind that you risk the wasting of time on such a shut-up dilatory correspondent. But on poetry there is so much to say, that I know not where to begin, & really wish to reply by a treatise of thirty sheets. I should like to be appointed your professor, you being required to attend the whole term. I should be very stern & exigeant, & insist on large readings & writings, & from haughty points of view. For a true lover of poetry must fly wide for his game, &, though the spirit of poetry is universal & is nearest, yet the successes of poets are scattered in all times & nations, & only in single passages, or single lines or even words; nay, the best are sometimes in writers of prose. But I did not mean to begin my inaugural discourse on this note; but only sat down to say that I find I am coming to New York in the beginning of next week, & I rely on your giving me an hour, & on your being docile, & concealing all your impatience of your tutor, nay, on your inspiring him by telling him your own results."

If a young girl receives such a letter from a great man—is it any wonder she cannot sleep nights for pride and ambition? Anyhow Emma seems to have written Emerson letters at such a rate that he—who was not cold, but old, who was overburdened and had to spare himself—could not keep pace with her. More and more he had to excuse himself for making her wait for his opinion of her poetry—and twice over when she was patient: "I have been looking in these weeks for a letter from you renouncing & denouncing me as a person incapable of all friendship, contumacious, &, in sum, a borrower of precious manuscripts which he neither publishes nor restores nor accounts for. Not having received such a letter, your patience & magnanimity rise daily to my wonder, &, at last, to my rebuke: And though by no means ready to send you my final Report on the duties with which I was charged, I will at least assure you that both the Manuscripts are safe, & by no means forgotten by me." But it is unimportant how often he wrote to her. Far more important is it that Emma could never doubt the sincerity of the advice he gave her in his letters. Chief evidence of this was his not merely praising but also finding fault with her productions. Every single line Emma wrote she sent to Concord. And Emerson, in his replies, examined everything in microscopic detail. She must not say 'gainst when the word was against, he admonished. Words like "intense" he found too shallow; they were not appropriate to the profundities of poetry. Sometimes he accused her of using "heedless words." "Doubt" was capable of many evils, but since when could doubt "ravage," he demanded.

His criticism, for all its sometimes whimsical tone, kept Emma on tenterhooks. In general he wanted her to write like himself (and this is a well-meant failing), with complete intellectual command of the passions, as one who had taken the measure of past ages without harm to himself and who lived with a full consciousness of what the present signified. Therefore he liked in Emma's writing a certain facility and smoothness that she had derived from him. But sometimes she seemed to him too smooth. He was particularly dissatisfied with a poem she wrote on Thoreau: "I do not think it cost you any day-dawn, or midnight oil." For in the final analysis Emerson knew very well that the greatest ease in art is hard won.

In the spring of 1868 Emerson himself had come to New York. But he had proved very nervous, for while he was forced by his lecture tours to do much traveling, he never felt at ease when he was away from home. Instead of having a searching talk with his protégé, he seems to have confined himself to recommending books—as in that letter where he suggested the reading of "Marcus Antoninus" (by which, of course, he meant Marcus Aurelius' *Meditations*). He also suggested the Sanskrit *Bhagavad-Gita,* and a recently published American book entitled *Man's Origin and Destiny.* It was a peculiarly Emersonian assortment—one day he would add Plato's *Theages*—and for the first time Emma realized that she would have preferred a conversation about more personal matters than books. Perhaps it was not true after all that the personal lives of human beings were only material for the making of good books. For that matter,

Emerson had already indicated in the course of the correspondence that books alone were not always sufficient. "Books are tools and seldom more. . . . Books are a safe ground, & a long one, but still introductory only, for what we really seek is ever comparison of experiences—to know if you have found therein what alone I prize, or still better if you have found what I have never found, & yet is admirable to me also."

On November 19, 1868, she sent him her second work in manuscript. It was *Admetus*, the mythological story of the woman who sacrificed herself for her husband. Admetus is doomed to die—but his wife goes to Hades in his place. A curious subject for a young girl, is it not? She still had her whole life before her, but already she was practicing the gestures of leavetaking. This in itself might be understandable. But the queer thing is that her Alcestis welcomes her death. Does not this give rise to the suspicion that the poet herself found life not very worth while? She seemed to underestimate her own personality, seeing it as the life of a mere woman, of a thoroughly feminine nature, in a world where only the actions of men are valued.

There is a curious significance in this. In Moses Lazarus' house there was a surplus of women. Only a single male heir was still living, Eliezer Frank, who was now eighteen years old. Two boys had died, or rather never lived: in August 1841 the first male child was stillborn and in August 1857 another son died at birth. The result was a "shortage of men" which brought the value of the man of the family up too high. Even so beloved a daughter as Emma felt this in her inmost soul. Otherwise she would not have selected this particular subject, an Alcestis who sacrifices herself for her husband because she undervalues herself.

But the subject revenged itself upon her. It was as if the content paralyzed the form. For the subject is so feminine that—out of compassion for the woman alone—a chivalrous man would almost inevitably create a better work and one with deeper spiritual insight. This was done by Euripides and in modern times by William Morris and Rainer Maria Rilke, whose finest short epic was devoted to Admetus and Alcestis.

Emerson at first saw nothing of this. His response to Emma's parcel was unconditional acclaim. After apparently having let the work lie for three weeks (he complained half-jestingly that "I have noble friends—they send me high poetry—pictures of gods, heroes & woman bravely & adequately drawn"), he burst out on November 19, 1868: "My dear friend, I write immediately on closing my first entire reading of 'Admetus,' to say, All Hail! You have written a noble poem, which I cannot enough praise. You have hid yourself from me until now, for the merits of the preceding poems did not unfold this fulness & high equality of power. I shall not stop to criticise, more than to say that it is too good than that the reader should feel himself *detained* by speeches a line too long. And the only suggestion I dare offer is that you shall read for the tone of Teutonic humanity Act III. Scene 1. of 'Measure for Measure,' as the only corrective of your classic sympathies. I think I shall return the treasured sheets by tomorrow's mail, secure that the eternal Apollo and the placated Fates will guard them to you."

In the abovementioned scene of *Measure for Measure* the imprisoned Claudio gives utterance to his dread of death in these terrible words:

> Ay, but to die, and go we know not where;
> To lie in cold obstruction, and to rot;
> This sensible warm motion to become
> A kneaded clod; and the delighted spirit

> To bathe in fiery floods or to reside
> In thrilling region of thick-ribbed ice;
> To be imprison'd in the viewless winds,
> And blown with restless violence round about
> The pendent world; or to be worse than worst
> Of those that lawless and incertain thoughts
> Imagine howling!—'tis too horrible!

It was not Emma's fault that she could not write such words—for, in fact, what man since Shakespeare could have written them? Yet Emerson's wanting to know that she had at least *read* them shows that Alcestis' readiness to die probably seemed to him too easy and Emma's "classical sympathies" too smooth.

He uttered nothing further of this sort. However, in August 1869, when Emma wanted to dedicate this second book of hers to him, Emerson grew hesitant. We do not know why. Possibly he was being altogether honest when he wrote to her that he would no longer be able to recommend the poem to others if it were dedicated to him. "If I am honored with the dedication my mouth is estopped." Nevertheless, she did dedicate it to him, and the dedication reveals her conception of this relationship which was the pride of her life. "To my friend, Ralph Waldo Emerson," she wrote. Not, say, "To my revered teacher," but simply, "To my friend." For the correspondence had already become a conversation between two friends who stood on the same level (though today we realize that Emerson always wrote with condescension).

8

In the volume, entitled *Admetus and Other Poems*, Emma had included together with the title poem several other verse narratives: "Orpheus," "Lohengrin" and "Tannhäuser." "Lohengrin" seems an exceptionally feeble piece, toying with dreams without substance, half derived from Rossetti, half Wagneresque.

> Complete in glittering silver armor clad,
> With silver-maiden shield, blank of device,
> Sir Lohengrin rode down the Montsalvatch,
> With Percivale and Tristram, Frimutelle
> And Eliduc, to speed him on his quest.
> They fared in silence, for the elder knights
> Were filled with grave misgivings, solemn thoughts
> Of fate and sorrow, and they heard the bell
> Tolling incessant; while Sir Lohengrin,
> Buoyant with hope, and dreaming like a girl,
> With wild blood dancing in his veins, had made
> The journey down the mount unconsciously,
> Surprised to find that he had reached the vale.
> Distinct and bowered in green the mountain loomed,
> Topped with the wondrous temple, with its cross
> Smitten to splendor by the eastern sun.
> Around them lay the valley beautiful,
> Imparadised with flowers and light of June;
> And through the valley flowed a willowy stream,
> Golden and gray, at this delicious hour,
> With purity and sunshine.

There is a hollow prettiness about this; it sounds like a school theme based on a pre-Raphaelite painting. This love for the "sweet" and this preference for a certain "emptiness" even enters a good poem like "Epochs," which otherwise is rich in thoughts. (It is based upon Emerson's motto: "The epochs of our life are not in the visible facts, but in the silent thought by the wayside as we walk.")

> Sweet empty sky of June without a stain,
>   Faint, gray-blue dewy mists on far-off hills,
> Warm, yellow sunlight flooding mead and plain,
>   That each dark copse and hollow overfills;
>   The rippling laugh of unseen, rain-fed rills,
> Weeds delicate-flowered, white and pink and gold,
>   A murmur and a singing manifold.

In "Tannhäuser," on the other hand, Emma, the stainless child, discovers at last that a "stained life," too, can be worthy of being lived. "Tannhäuser," remarkably, stands on a higher level than the other verse narratives. But if it does so, it is not because of the person of Venus, not because of that type of "perfect beauty" which (as the only thing which would counterbalance woman's weakness in a manmade world) would become so increasingly important in Emma's later years. Contrariwise, the atmosphere of the Venusberg with its "smell of spice and roses, frankincense and balm" is hard to breathe, and the whole bacchanal, with its jeweled and scintillating ballet of the Venus followers is rather bad painting. Tannhäuser's character has remarkable depths. Later on, when the unhappy knight, after his damnation by the Pope, staggers home from Rome, he finds some thoughts by the wayside which are not unworthy of the later Emma Lazarus, of her crusades against intolerance and her love for her human "fellow-sufferers."

> Vague thoughts and gleams prophetic filled his brain.
> "Ah, fool!" he mused, "to look for help from men.
> Had they the will to aid, they lack the power.
> In mine own flesh and soul the sin had birth,
> Through mine own anguish it must be atoned.
> Our saviors are not saints and ministers,
> But tear-strung women, children soft of heart,
> Or fellow-sufferers, who, by some chance word,

Some glance of comfort, save us from despair.
These I have found, thank Heaven! to strengthen trust
In mine own kind, when all the world grew dark.
Make me not proud in spirit, O my God!
Yea, in thy sight I am one mass of sin,
One black and foul corruption, yet I know
My frailty is exceeded by thy love.
Neither is this the slender straw of hope,
Whereto I, drowning, cling, but firm belief,
That fills my inmost soul with vast content.
As surely as the hollow faiths of old
Shriveled to dust before one ray of Truth,
So will these modern temples pass away,
Piled upon rotten doctrines, baseless forms,
And man will look in his own breast for help,
Yea, search for comfort his own inward reins,
Revere himself, and find the God within."

But in spite of this and in spite of "Marjorie's Wooing," a fine piece in the manner of the Scottish folk ballads, we might perhaps dismiss Emma's productions as the typical "second book" of a former child prodigy if the volume did not also contain her extraordinarily successful translation of the first act of Goethe's *Faust*. With true artist's instinct Emma saw how to convert Goethe's verses into the English equivalent. The twenty-one-year-old girl broke up the medieval form derived from Hans Sachs, the *Knüttelvers* or doggerel (for a parallel form in English she should have had to borrow from Chaucer) and boldly transposed it all into the style of the Renaissance, into Elizabethan iambics that are replete with the vigor of modern action. (The reward of such success was that for decades Emma's reputation was merely that of an excellent translator.)

To rob Goethe of his *rhymes* was a hazardous enterprise

and perhaps even a crime to German ears. But let us see how she performed the task. —It is night. In a narrow, vaulted Gothic chamber we behold the old, bearded Faust and hear his immortal lament:

> I have, alas! by zealous energy
> Mastered philosophy and medicine,
> With law, and, woe is me! theology;
> Yet grow, poor fool, no wiser than before.
> They call me Master, yea, and Doctor too;
> For nine years I have led my pupils round,
> By crooked ways and straight, and to and fro,
> And see at last that nothing can be known.
> This thought will break my heart! 'Tis true, indeed,
> I am more clever than the solemn fools,
> The doctors, authors, magistrates, and priests.
> No doubts nor scruples vex me. I fear not
> Hell nor the Devil; therefore joy is dead.
> I dream no more my knowledge valuable,—
> I dream no longer I can teach mankind
> Aught to ennoble or to elevate.
> Besides, I have not either money, lands,
> Honor, nor rank: no dog would live like this!
> So I devote myself to magic arts.
> Perchance, through power of the soul and voice,
> Many a mystery will be clear to me,
> So that no longer I, with bitter sweat,
> Must speak of what I do not understand;
> So that I may discover what that is
> That holds the world together at its heart,
> See all the germs and forces of creation,
> And drive no more a petty trade with words.

True, to a connoisseur of the German original Emma's use of iambic pentameter must have meant the entering of something of a "prosaic element." But see what Goethe's verses, by losing some of their "genuine poesy," have gained in dramatic speed:

> Overhead,
> The sky is clouded and the moon concealed,
> The lamp-light flickers, noisome grows the air,
> Red rays flash round my head, a tremor falls
> From the high vault, and makes my flesh to creep.
> I feel thee, thou art near me, spirit charmed
> By prayer. Unveil! Alas, my heart is torn,
> With strange emotions is my being thrilled;
> I feel my whole soul given up to thee,—
> Thou must! thou must! though it should cost my life!
>
> (*He seizes the book and repeats the incantation mystically. A rosy flame flashes up, and the spirit appears in the flame.*)
> SPIRIT.
> Who calls me?

9

Emerson's letters to Emma Lazarus—treasured in the manuscript room of the library of Columbia University and edited in 1939 by one of our best Emerson scholars, Ralph L. Rusk —do not mention the *Faust* translation. But on June 7, 1869, the writer of the letters discloses which poem of Emma's he most preferred. It was "Heroes"—the poem Emma had dedicated to those who had died in and to those who had survived the Civil War—and this time Emerson's taste was unerringly right. When he received the manuscript and read it for the first time, he rushed upstairs and read it to his wife and to his daughter Ellen—"the voice falters," he wrote her, "in reading it aloud":

In rich Virginian woods,
The scarlet creeper reddens over graves,
Among the solemn trees enlooped with vines;
Heroic spirits haunt the solitudes,—
The noble souls of half a million braves,
  Amid the murmurous pines.

. . . .

Here, though all seems at peace,
The placid, measureless sky serenely fair,
The laughter of the breeze among the leaves,
The bars of sunlight slanting through the trees,
The reckless wild-flowers blooming everywhere,
  The grasses' delicate sheaves,—

Nathless each breeze that blows,
Each tree that trembles to its leafy head
With nervous life, revives within our mind,
Tender as flowers of May, the thoughts of those
Who lie beneath the living beauty, dead,—
  Beneath the sunshine, blind.

. . . .

But who has sung their praise,
Not less illustrious, who are living yet?
Armies of heroes, satisfied to pass
Calmly, serenely from the whole world's gaze,
And cheerfully accept, without regret,
  Their old life as it was,

With all its petty pain,
Its irritating littleness and care;
They who have scaled the mountain, with content
Sublime, descend to live upon the plain;
Steadfast as though they breathed the mountain-air
  Still, whereso'er they went.

They who were brave to act,
And rich enough their action to forget;
Who, having filled their day with chivalry,
Withdraw and keep their simpleness intact,
And all unconscious add more lustre yet
   Unto their victory.

On the broad Western plains
Their patriarchal life they live anew;
Hunters as mighty as the men of old,
Or harvesting the plenteous, yellow grains,
Gathering ripe vintage of dusk bunches blue,
   Or working mines of gold;

Or toiling in the town,
Armed against hindrance, weariness, defeat,
With dauntless purpose not to swerve or yield,
And calm, defiant strength, they struggle on,
As sturdy and as valiant in the street,
   As in the camp and field.

.   .   .   .

   New England fields I see,
The lovely, cultured landscape, waving grain,
Wide, haughty rivers, and pale, English skies.
And lo! a farmer ploughing busily,
Who lifts a swart face, looks upon the plain,—
   I see, in his frank eyes,

The hero's soul appear.
Thus in the common fields and streets they stand;
The light that on the past and distant gleams,
They cast upon the present and the near,
With antique virtues from some mystic land,
   Of knightly deeds and dreams.

"... it is the first time it has been said in America," Ellen Emerson commented. She grew so fond of the poem that she made copies and had them sent to Lieutenant Colonel W. H. Forbes and Captain Charles Emerson, and to other friends and relatives. The poem won everyone by its heartfelt warmth and utter absence of rhetoric—and yet not everyone: Emma, whose ear was far more sensitive to criticism than to praise, learned from Emerson that James Russell Lowell had said that "by rough judgment" she could be driven "to a severer pruning of her verses."

She had a deep veneration for the poet Lowell. His war poem, "The Washers of the Shroud," written in October 1861, with its mysterious revival of the Norns who decide the destinies of nations, was well known to her. As she later pointed out to her London friends, Lowell's poem had stanzas that before him only Lord Byron could have written:

"Still men and nations reap as they have strawn,"
So sang they, working at their task the while;
"The fatal raiment must be cleansed ere dawn:
For Austria? Italy? the Sea-Queen's isle?
O'er what quenched grandeur must our shroud be drawn?

"Or is it for a younger, fairer Corse,
That gathered States like children round his knees,
That tamed the wave to be his posting-horse,
Feller of forests, linker of the seas,
Bridge-builder, hammerer, youngest son of Thor's?"

The penultimate stanza, however, Emma loved to recite aloud:

"God, give us peace! not such as lulls to sleep,
But sword on thigh, and brow with purpose knit!
And let our Ship of State to harbor sweep,
Her ports all up, her battle-lanterns lit,
And her leashed thunders gathering for their leap!"

Emma, a woman, for the present could not write in *this* fashion. More time had to pass before she could discover sufficient strength in herself for the heroic. Her "Heroes," after all, was the work of a womanly spirit.

But what Lowell's opinion of her verses was at that time is perhaps not so important as Emerson's having spoken to him of Emma Lazarus at all. It has occasionally been thought that Emerson's interest in Emma had been that of a kind of private tutor. This is entirely wrong. He often spoke of her talent to other people. Even before *Admetus* appeared in book form, he had recommended it to another leading figure of American letters, William Dean Howells. Emerson gave it to Howells with the suggestion that it be published in advance in the *Atlantic Monthly*.

If Ralph Waldo Emerson was the greatest cosmopolitan of his age, Howells, thirty years his junior, represented the European sensibility brought to bear on the American scene. Howells had only recently returned to Boston from his consular service in Venice. The high level of his critical writings was the result of his precise knowledge of English, French and Italian literature. If Emma Lazarus' *Admetus* had been signed by one of the recognized poets of Victorian England, Howells would probably have termed it one of the weaker poems of a good writer and would not have rejected it. Curiously enough, three years later, Emma's *Admetus* was well received in England. The widely circulated *Illustrated London News*, hitting out even at the great Robert Browning, made this astonishing comment: "In her treatment of the story of 'Admetus' . . . she is far happier than Mr. Browning in his half adaption of Euripides. . . . The conflicts . . . are represented with more force as well as grace in this poem than in that of Mr. Browning. It will be no surprise to us, after the present volume, if Miss Lazarus hereafter takes a high place among the best poets in this age of our common English tongue."

But this was yet to come. When in 1869 Emerson sent the unprinted *Admetus* to Howells, unfortunately for Emma this *arbiter elegantiarum* had never heard of her. He rejected *Admetus*, writing somewhat insultingly that he saw nothing original in it at all, that it was an imitative work in the style of Lord Alfred Tennyson and William Morris.

Emerson was too well-mannered to pass on this verdict. He not only softened the blow for Emma, but expressly deplored Howell's decision not to print *Admetus:* "I should have printed it thankfully & proudly. . . . I am at a loss to find the imitation of Tennyson & Morris that the editor remarks. I am glad you had the courage & diligence to condense the piece, and now the more, that our Aristarchus," as he mockingly called the severe critic, "still finds you too expansive." But the most important thing was his pointing out to Emma—a valuable lesson!—how whimsical and uncertain a thing was the "literary taste" that dictated such Jupiter-like decisions.

Nevertheless, after the appearance of the second book (and even before), their correspondence flagged. In the early summer of 1869 Emma had written to him that one of her uncles (her mother's brother Benjamin, a son of Seixas Nathan) had been slain in a holdup in New York. Emerson's answer, of course, expressed his horror. "I had seen the bulletin in the journals without a suspicion that it touched any friend of mine. You know how the eye learns to rush over these records of outrages which we cannot hinder or in any manner repair." The extraordinarily frank confession of a man who did not care to be touched by the sorrows of others. And he immediately said why. "I know how we hate and shun the dismal. It seems rather to lead *from* than *to* thought, and so wastes the Soul." It was only by the roundabout way of one of his half-optimistic, half-stoical clichés ("that doleful tract is part also of the Universe") that he happened to say to her that there is good in evil, too.

Did not Emma suspect anything when, in the next years, their correspondence dwindled to a trickle? She had no forebodings; she in fact suspected nothing. But then, a few years later, something happened that she would have thought impossible. Emerson had been quietly preparing a huge book, an anthology of English poetry running to almost a thousand columns. The book was to be unique, for in it English and American poems were going to be printed side by side for the first time. In other words, for the first time the American offspring were to be introduced into the ancient, aristocratic English family. This book was to present one indivisible body of poetry beginning more than four hundred years ago with Chaucer and Shakespeare, and continuing on down to the present day with poets who resided in Birmingham or Boston.

Parnassus was the title of the book. When Emma Lazarus first looked through it, she could scarcely believe her eyes. She was a profoundly modest person and had never seriously thought that she belonged in a book containing whole pages of Shakespeare and poems by Burns and Byron. But were her own poems really inferior to those of Henry Howard Barnes, William Cullen Bryant (who had only recently praised her work), N. L. Frothingham, Bret Harte, Oliver Wendell Holmes, Julia Ward Howe or that mysterious H. H. who for some reason wished to remain anonymous?

People from Boston, New York, Philadelphia—contemporaries who seemed to have no special intellectual advantage over her—what was there about their poems that Emerson should single them out? All of them were in his book, a book so spacious that he was hard put to find enough material for all of its nine hundred columns.

Certainly she belonged there! Certainly there was room in this book for her proud poem "How Long," written in 1871. Emerson knew the poem very well; in it she had turned away from the Anglomania of her own childhood.

> How long, and yet how long,
> Our leaders will we hail from over seas,
> Masters and kings from feudal monarchies,
>   And mock their ancient song
> With echoes weak of foreign melodies?
>
> That distant isle mist-wreathed,
> Mantled in unimaginable green,
> Too long hath been our mistress and our queen.
>   Our fathers have bequeathed
> Too deep a love for her, our hearts within.
>
> She made the whole world ring
> With the brave exploits of her children strong,
> And with the matchless music of her song.
>   Too late, too late we cling
> To alien legends, and their strains prolong.
>
> This fresh young world I see,
> With heroes, cities, legends of her own;
> With a new race of men, and overblown
>   By winds from sea to sea,
> Decked with the majesty of every zone.
>
> I see the glittering tops
> Of snow-peaked mounts, the wid'ning vale's expanse
> Large prairies where free herds of horses prance,
>   Exhaustless wealth of crops,
> In vast, magnificent extravagance.

> These grand, exuberant plains,
> These stately rivers, each with many a mouth,
> The exquisite beauty of the soft-aired south,
>   The boundless seas of grains,
> Luxuriant forests' lush and splendid growth.
>
> The distant siren-song
> Of the green island in the eastern sea,
> Is not the lay for this new chivalry,
>   It is not free and strong
> To chant on prairies 'neath this brilliant sky.
>
> The echo faints and fails;
> It suiteth not, upon this western plain,
> Our voice or spirit; we should stir again
>   The wilderness, and make the vales
> Resound unto a yet unheard-of strain.

Was not this anthology just the place for such verses, where they were destined to stand in their American pride face to face with the matchless songs of the elder isle?

Emma did not see that Walt Whitman, too, had been excluded from *Parnassus*. It seemed to her, it could not help seeming to her, that her name alone was missing. It was inexplicable why Emerson had done this to her who had been so faithful to him. But it had been done and it was the greatest betrayal of her life, one comparable to a broken engagement, but a more heinous crime. He had espoused and loved her verses—and now he had thrown them over.

10

Emma suffered a complete breakdown.

The house at 36 West Fourteenth Street where she had lived and written her poetry, from which she had sent her letters to Emerson, seemed bleak and lightless to her now. She sat without speaking, her clasped hands in her lap. Her parents, sisters, and brother tried unsuccessfully to console her. What, after all, had happened? She had been left out of a book, that was all. It was easy for them to talk, but Emma Lazarus knew better. Although she did not know the laws of fame, the meaningless chance and mechanical absurdity by which those laws operated, she felt at the bottom of her heart that being left out of the anthology was more than a mere wound to her vanity. It was a blow directed at her whole poetic being, a blow from which it might well take her decades to recover.

Did she guess right and was it so important? It was, for there really are certain books in which a young writer must have a place if his later reputation is not to suffer. And Emerson's anthology was one such book. Anyone who was omitted from it in 1875 would have faint chance of maintaining a name in 1900, and by 1925 he would be quite forgotten. Emerson, to be sure, would have denied this. In one of his best essays, "Spiritual Laws," he had written: "A man passes for that he is worth. Very idle is all curiosity concerning other people's estimate of us, and all fear of remaining unknown is not less so. If a man know that he can do any thing,—that he can do it better than any one else,—he has a pledge of the acknowledgement of that fact by all persons. The world is full of judgment-days; and into every assembly that a man enters, in every action he attempts, he is gauged and stamped." But this does not hold true at all for literature. There are very few judgment days indeed, and critics senselessly reiterate their predecessors' verdicts. Exclusion from an anthology which purported to contain all the contemporary verse worth printing was virtually equivalent to a death sentence. Once again that injustice had been done which is repeated in every generation: a large number of talented persons no worse than others do not emerge from obscurity only because they missed an opportunity. (Emerson's naivety in matters of fame was so great that once, when Emma was reading some poems by Charles De Kay to him and she remarked: "Isn't it a pity that he has so small an audience?" Emerson gave her a look of astonishment and countered: "Why? In this very moment he has you and he has me.")

Now, after the lapse of seventy-five years, one wishes one might ask Emma why she wept. Did she not see what an unpoetic thing this anthology of poetry was? Look at these classifications into which have been crammed four hundred years of poetry: I. Nature. II. Human Life. III. Intellectual. IV. Contemplative. V. Heroic. VI. Portraits and Pictures. VII. Narrative Poems and Ballads. VIII. Songs. IX. Dirges and Pathetic Poems. X. Comic and Humorous. XI. Poetry of Terror. XII. Oracles and Counsels. Now, did she really think that this kind of bureaucratic classification did justice to the spirit of the poets in the book?

It is easy to say this. But Emma would have replied with the dignity of the insulted: "Still I should like to have had a place in it, unpoetic as it may have been. Why? Because the others are in it."

She wrote him a despairing letter which he did not even answer! Perhaps he did not write because, buried as he had been for years under a mountain of English manuscripts, he had really only forgotten Emma. This she could have accepted; because of the shock he had experienced after the partial burning of his house in 1872, his memory failed him more and more. She knew that he could even forget that a poet named Poe had lived. For Poe, too, was not in *Parnassus*! But no, she could not accept this interpretation. The omission could not have been accidental; it must have been a conscious condemnation of her writing! Emerson must have decided that William Dean Howells had been right after all in rejecting her work! For a time he had liked seeing the verses—old men have a weakness for versifying girls. But she would write no more poetry, perhaps there were more useful things to do in a world of which Dorothea Schlegel, the daughter of Moses Mendelssohn, had said, bitterly but sensibly: "Really, there are too many books, but I have never heard that there were too many shirts. . . ." What, then, about needle and thread, Miss Emma Lazarus?

The wound did not heal, but its existence gave depth to her character. If Emma was to go on writing, she would no longer tolerate such family jokes as Josephine's (untrue) remark: "Just imagine, Emma has written all of fifteen hundred stanzas in two weeks." She realized that rhythm had often seduced her, that her poetry had come too easily to her. How would it be to try prose?

In Goethe's *Dichtung und Wahrheit* she had read about the Sesenheim episode. Young Goethe had loved Friederike Brion and left her. Around this romantic situation with its psychological overtones, Emma had written a carefully constructed novel, *Alide*. Although she had had no similar experience in her own life—for she had begun the novel a year before her break with Emerson—she identified herself with the abandoned Friederike.

11

What is a novel—or, rather, what should it be? "A work in which the greatest powers of the mind are displayed, in which the most thorough knowledge of human nature, the happiest delineation of its varieties, the liveliest effusions of wit and humor are conveyed to the world in the best chosen language."

If Jane Austen (after one of whose heroines Emma had

been named) is right in saying this, then Emma's novel was not a good one. She did not yet possess a thorough knowledge of human nature, nor was the theme itself the best one to call forth her greatest powers of mind. Alide sounds not unlike Alcestis. The same theme crops up: woman is nothing beside man. The inferiority feelings that sprang from her family situation, which had begun to affect her relations to men, were already shaping Emma's writing.

When the novel was published she did not send it to Emerson (at any rate there is no evidence that she did), but to a European novelist living in Paris whom she revered, Ivan Turgeniev, one of the greatest prose writers of the Slavic world. At that time he was filled with strangely mixed feelings of love and hatred toward all things Russian. Without having been exiled himself, he sometimes acted like an *exilé*. Henry James' book *French Poets and Novelists*, which Emma was to hold in high regard, had not yet appeared (it came out a few years later, in 1878) but she, too, esteemed Turgeniev as a Frenchman rather than as a Russian. She had read his books (at least his *Fathers and Sons* [1862] and *Smoke* [1867]) either in English or in French—novels of which she said, that they were "solid earth, but with iridescent clouds above."

Although the master had yet to put the finishing touches to his famous novel *Virgin Soil*, he read *Alide* at once. He replied with a certain reserve, but with sincere praise. ". . . though, generally speaking, I do not think it advisable to take celebrated modern men—especially poets and artists—as a subject for a novel—still I am truly glad to say that I have read your book with the liveliest interest: It is very sincere and very poetical at the same time; the life and spirit of Germany have no secrets for you—and your characters are drawn with a pencil as delicate as it is strong.— I feel very proud of the approbation you give to my works

—and of the influence you kindly attribute to them on your own talent: an author, who writes as you do—is not a 'pupil in art' any more; he is not far from being himself a master."

Turgeniev had surely meant what he had written, and two years later confirmed in a second letter what he had said. But we are a bit puzzled today by his praise and by the sympathetic things he said about Emma and her novel to Thomas Wentworth Higginson. Turgeniev, whose education had been in part a German one, was naturally an excellent Goethe student, and at once recognized that Emma Lazarus had taken whole passages from Goethe's autobiography into *Alide*. He did not need to read the explicit statement Emma had made in her preface: "Wherever it has been possible, he [Goethe] has been allowed to speak for himself, and thus no imagination has been exercised in the portrayal of his character." Turgeniev had probably in truth been touched by the "sincere" and "poetical" in that questionable novel, and perhaps, too, by Emma's more than polite reference to his influence on her. Her novel did indeed show some of his influence.

When a few years before Henry T. Tuckerman had written of Emma's "spiritual and musical gifts," he had not mentioned her gift for painting landscapes in words, for the good reason that it was hardly apparent in her work before she set foot on English soil in 1883. But in *Alide* this talent is in evidence. We come across it in the scene where Goethe, wanting to surprise Alide, sets out in disguise to see her.

". . . after passing beyond the hedges of the village gardens, he was embarrassed by seeing some country-people advancing towards him along the footpath. By his side was a hill crowned by a small wood, and, springing up the elevation, he plunged into the grove, in order to conceal himself till the appointed time. He found himself at once in a little sylvan paradise. The soft turf was mottled with broken sunlight and strewn with the first fall of leaves; patches of the deep-blue sky were shining between the restless foliage and waving branches, and on every side a heaven-bright picture, set in a bushy frame, opened before him. Below, was the lively village and at no great distance, as seen from this point, stood the gray parsonage, embosomed in its prosperous fields. Beyond, lay Drusenheim, with its old-fashioned inn, and its glittering tiled roof that caught the sunlight, while far away rose into sight the steeple of Strasburg Minster. He could catch between the trees a glimpse of the flowing shimmer of the Rhine, and could distinguish in the hazy distance its woody islands, with their magical tints of yellow and russet and green. In the opposite direction waved the noble outlines of the Vosges, their purple hollows and dazzling light-green pasture-slopes streaked with shifting shadows."

Has this really been observed with the eyes of Goethe? Yes, it has—but Goethe here has profited by Turgeniev's acute observation of nature.

Emma's novel from its very first word, however, was marred by her total inexperience of the relations between the sexes. The coquettish arts with which a girl holds a man, for example, were entirely foreign to her. Friederike Brion's being too "serious" for Goethe has notoriously been made much of in the modern psychological literature on him (a good deal of it has recently been published in this country). Of course she was! And for a like reason—because Emma Lazarus was much too serious to comprehend so fickle a person as the young Goethe was and to portray him wittily and charmingly—the novel *Alide* failed. The novel has distinction only where the great theme of Emma's own youth crops up—the *dread of love*, dread of what the French call *l'abandon*. Fear of the faithlessness of men. There is a scene where Goethe (who was famous for his Shakespeare recitations) reads aloud from *Hamlet* at an evening gathering. From the way in which the loving Ophelia speaks of Hamlet, Alide suddenly perceived that Goethe did not love her, Alide. "And yet, though her attitude remained unchanged, and her hands lay quietly crossed in her lap, any one who had watched her attentively would have seen that she was a prey to a succession of various and powerful emotions. From time to time she sighed deeply, and a passing color tinged her cheeks. . . . The blood fled from her eager face, her thin white fingers stirred convulsively, as she heard the wise, kind, chilling answer of Laertes:

>   Think it no more,
> For nature, crescent, does not grow alone
> In thews and bulk; but, as this temple waxes,
> The inward service of the mind and soul
> Grows wide withal.

A pathetic, bewildered expression clouded Alide's countenance, until soon, forgetful of herself and suddenly responsive to some lofty thought, some heroic passion, the light and color rippled again over brow and cheek, and a faint smile of irrepressible delight played upon her lips."

This, really, was Emma herself. And it was to this virgin soul, infected by a lifelong fear of being jilted, that so terrible a thing as the *Parnassus* incident had happened! It was unforgettable and seemed unpardonable—but Turgeniev's letter, and some others equally commendatory, not to forget the very friendly reception literary circles gave *Alide*, restored Emma's self-assurance. And now Emma Lazarus did something that is to her credit as a person and as a woman: she apparently resumed her correspondence with Ralph Waldo Emerson without even alluding to the matter that had given her so much heartache. The "forgetful old man," who after all (something *we* must not forget) had seen her only a few times in his life, would seem to have felt a half-conscious guilt toward her. It is curious that Emerson—as Ralph L. Rusk reports—wrote down the address of the Lazarus family in his notebook when he went from Massachusetts to Philadelphia to deliver a lecture in the spring of 1876. Did he intend to pay a call at Moses Lazarus' home in New York? We do not know. But, in any case, in this summer of 1876 Emerson and his wife invited Emma to Concord.

12

A journey from New York to Concord—what an adventure that was! In 1876 Emma was twenty-seven years old, but we can be fairly certain that she had never yet traveled alone or spent even a single day away from her family. And she would not have been permitted to travel now, had it not been for the invitation from Emerson's *wife*; there would be ladies present, after all, who could watch over her. Emma described it all in her diary: how Emerson himself (far older now than she had remembered him) was waiting for her at the railroad station, in his grave simplicity, and how he drove her to his home "in his little one-horse wagon to the gray square house with dark green blinds, amidst noble trees." On the porch she was received with open arms by "the stately, white-haired Mrs. Emerson, and the beautiful, faithful Ellen." The very first evening she felt strongly drawn to these women: this stranger's garden wafted a homelike fragrance to her nostrils. Emma felt intensely filial, not toward Emerson, but toward his wife, the mother.

Only a few months ago Emma had lost her own mother. For the first time death had torn out one link of the close-knit family. Perhaps this visit would never have been made if Hettie Lazarus had still been alive. But Emma discovered that the memory of her mother revived more strongly than ever in the presence of a woman who represented a good mother.

These matters were delicately touched on when the Emersons walked through the August mowings with Emma Lazarus and watched the midsummer sunsets. Emma was refreshed by this odd garden town where so many poets lived. The voice of the trees, whose mingled melodies entered through her window morning and evening, reminded her of a soul who was no longer here—Thoreau. And from day to day the deceased Thoreau came to matter more to her than the living Emerson. She began to see faults in Emerson that she had never noticed before. She saw, for example, that philosophy was essential to him, but that he could exist entirely without music. And his way of speaking, the somewhat preacherly and rhetorical tone, even though it was softened by age, now alienated her somewhat—as she later confessed to English friends.

But Thoreau! It seemed to her as though his face, his eyes, his beard, his brow had sunk back into the landscape; he dwelt in the woods about Concord. And his faithful disciple was here, the poet William Ellery Channing, who was ready at any time to talk about Thoreau. Speaking of Emma's reaction to Channing, Josephine Lazarus, in her introduction to the *Poems*, says that his "figure stands out like a gnarled and twisted scrub-oak,—a pathetic, impossible creature, whose cranks and oddities were submitted to on account of an innate nobility of character." With warm feeling, but keen insight Emma wrote in her diary: "Generally crabbed and reticent with strangers, he took a liking to me. . . . The bond of our sympathy was my admiration for Thoreau . . . I do not know whether I was most touched by the thought of the unique, lofty character that had inspired this depth and fervor of friendship, or by the pathetic constancy and pure affection of the poor, desolate old man before me, who tried to conceal his tenderness and sense of irremediable loss. . . . He never speaks of Thoreau's death, but always 'Thoreau's loss,' or 'when I lost Mr. Thoreau,' or 'when Mr. Thoreau went away from Concord'; nor would he confess that he missed him, for there was not a day, an hour, a moment when he did not feel that his friend was still with him and had never left him. And yet a day or two after when I sat with him in the sunlit wood looking at the gorgeous blue and silver summer sky, he turned to me and said: 'Just half of the world died for me when I lost Mr. Thoreau. None of it looks the same as when I looked at it with him.' . . . He took me through the woods and pointed out to me every spot visited and described by his friend. Where the hut stood is a little pile of stones and a sign, 'Site of Thoreau's Hut,' and a few steps beyond is the pond with thickly-wooded shores,—everything exquisitely peaceful and beautiful in the afternoon light, and not a sound to be heard except the crickets or the 'z-ing' of the locusts which Thoreau has described. Farther on he pointed out to me, in the distant landscape, a low roof, the only one visible, which was the roof of Thoreau's birthplace. He had been over there many times, he said, since he lost Mr. Thoreau, but had never gone in,—he was afraid it might look lonely! But he had often sat on a rock in front of the house and looked at it." ("If Channing could only have written as he talked . . . New England would have had its Virgil," Van Wyck Brooks later said of similar scenes.)

Thoreau had been one of "life's eremites," a saint of solitude—and therein lay his uniqueness. Emerson, although in his innermost soul he too despised society, was a preacher and teacher who exercised great influence upon people and was in turn influenced by them. But for Emma there ceased to be (at least, for a long time) any comparison between the two after she had made the acquaintance of both in Concord, the living man and the shade.

When she left, Channing, with a furtive expression, handed her a small package. She was not to open it, he whispered, until she was on the train. When she undid the package she found in it a copy of the book he had written on Thoreau, and, in addition, a relic. It was the pocket compass that the hermit poet had used during his tramps through the woods. Emma looked thoughtfully down at the instrument. She was returning to the metropolis where a compass was of no use. Nevertheless, in the general way of life one stood badly in need of a compass. Only, she may have felt, life was far more perilous than all the woods of Massachusetts and Maine that Henry Thoreau had loved.

13

It would have been unnatural for Emma not to talk with Emerson about her work; moreover, avoiding the topic would have given her away. Her whole plan was based on her behaving as though nothing had happened. Yes, by all means she had to show him something she had written *after* the *Parnassus* incident.

A year before, Emma Lazarus had written a poem which for largeness of spirit and formal strength she was rarely to equal again. It was the ode "On the Proposal to Erect a Monument in England to Lord Byron." Ever since the anonymous teacher had implanted a love for English poetry in her child's heart, this poem had been secretly gathering within her; it burst forth one day when Emma read in a newspaper (1875) that England wished "to make good the wrong it had once done Lord Byron." Byron himself had conceived many a poem of his in a similar way: a newspaper report would unloose his anger or love and set his great creative force in motion. Emma's personality mingled with that of the dead poet in her ode. It is as if secret "insults" of her own lurked in the background: it all now vented itself in a catharsis of "Byronic indignation."

> The grass of fifty Aprils hath waved green
>   Above the spent heart, the Olympian head,
> The hands crost idly, the shut eyes unseen,
>   Unseeing, the locked lips whose song hath fled;
> Yet mystic-lived, like some rich, tropic flower,
> His fame puts forth fresh blossoms hour by hour;
> Wide spread the laden branches dropping dew
>   On the low, laureled brow misunderstood,
>   That bent not, neither bowed, until subdued
> By the last foe who crowned while he o'erthrew.

Byron, we must remember, died on Greek soil, and they were Greeks, not Englishmen, who stood beside his bier:

> Fair was the Easter Sabbath morn when first
>   Men heard he had not wakened to its light:
> The end had come, and time had done its worst,
>   For the black cloud had fallen of endless night.
> Then in the town, as Greek accosted Greek,
> 'Twas not the wonted festal words to speak,
> "Christ is arisen," but "Our chief is gone,"
>   With such wan aspect and grief-smitten head
>   As when the awful cry of "Pan is dead!"
> Filled echoing hill and valley with its moan.

> "I am more fit for death than the world deems,"
>   So spake he as life's light was growing dim,
> And turned to sleep as unto soothing dreams.
>   What terrors could its darkness hold for him,

Familiar with all anguish, but with fear
Still unacquainted? On his martial bier
They laid a sword, a helmet, and a crown—
    Meed of the warrior, but not these among
    His voiceless lyre, whose silent chords unstrung
Shall wait—how long?—for touches like his own.

An alien country mourned him as her son,
    And hailed him hero: his sole, fitting tomb
Were Theseus' temple or the Parthenon,
    Fondly she deemed. His brethren bare him home,
Their exiled glory, past the guarded gate
Where England's Abbey shelters England's great.
Afar he rests whose very name hath shed
    New lustre on her with the song he sings.
    So Shakespeare rests who scorned to lie with kings,
Sleeping at peace midst the unhonored dead.

And fifty years suffice to overgrow
    With gentle memories the foul weeds of hate
That shamed his grave. The world begins to know
    Her loss, and view with other eyes his fate.
Even as the cunning workman brings to pass
The sculptor's thought from out the unwieldy mass
Of shapeless marble, so Time lops away
    The stony crust of falsehood that concealed
    His just proportions, and, at last revealed,
The statue issues to the light of day,

Most beautiful, most human. Let them fling
    The first stone who are tempted even as he,
And have not swerved. When did that rare soul sing
    The victim's shame, the tyrant's eulogy,
The great belittle, or exalt the small,
Or grudge his gift, his blood, to disenthrall

The slaves of tyranny or ignorance?
   Stung by fierce tongues himself, whose rightful fame
   Hath he reviled? Upon what noble name
Did the winged arrows of that barbed wit glance?

The years' thick, clinging curtains backward pull,
   And show him as he is, crowned with bright beams,
"Beauteous, and yet not all as beautiful
   As he hath been or might be; Sorrow seems
Half of his immortality." He needs
No monument whose name and song and deeds
Are graven in all foreign hearts; but she
   His mother, England, slow and last to wake,
   Needs raise the votive shaft for her fame's sake:
Hers is the shame if such forgotten be!

If Emma had read this poem aloud to her friend in Concord, it would have probably, as Homer says, "pierced him through the temples." No critic's casque was stout enough not to let pass these verses. Although Emerson can by no means be called a "Byronian," and although in all likelihood he thought the same thing of Emma's liking for Byron as did William James, the philosopher of pragmatism, who later wrote this warning to her in a letter: "Don't you rather overdo Byron? Vide his life! And big and careless as is his power, isn't it essentially *rhetorical* power, the power of words that are often but echoes of other words . . ."—Yet this remarkable poem would have more convinced him of her ability than everything else he knew of her. But—it is on such accidents that larger things often hang—she had not brought the poem with her to Concord. Nor could she have brought the poem with her, for if she had shown it to him it would have seemed as if she were begging him to bear it in mind for some later edition of *Parnassus*. So now she did something else, something that proved not too fortunate. Although she must have seen how tired he looked, she showed him, almost casually, the proof sheets of her play, *The Spagnoletto*, which she had carried in her luggage intending to correct them during her stay at Concord. This seemed an inconsequential act, on an inconsequential evening.

14

She might have added at once that it was hardly intended for the stage. Neither Byron's Renaissance plays nor those of Robert Browning had been so intended. Emma did not expect Emerson to take it for anything but a closet drama. Next morning he returned the play to her, tersely remarking that he thought it "good." As Josephine later recounted, Emma then playfully asked him whether he would not give her a bigger word to take home to the family. He laughed and said he did not know of any, but he went on to tell her that he had taken it up not expecting to read it through, and had not been able to put it down. Every word and line showed the richness of the poetry, he said, and as far as he could judge the play had great dramatic potentialities.

Emerson knew no more about the theater than most of his disciples. The Concord writers devoted themselves to philosophy and lyric poetry, and occasionally to the novel, but not to the drama. It had been a mistake on Emma's part to show him this Renaissance tragedy whose locale was the Naples of 1665. For Emerson, though he had entitled one of his finest essays "History," in reality hated history. And no less than and exactly for the same reasons that his most famous disciple, Nietzsche, would hate history. As a motto of this essay Emerson had used the quatrain:

> I am owner of the sphere,
> Of the seven stars and the solar year,
> Of Caesar's hand, and Plato's brain,
> Of Lord Christ's heart, and Shakespeare's strain.

These were words of warning, a warning to the past that it had in itself no objective life; it existed only insofar as a contemporary mind saw points of interest in it. It was precisely this extreme subjectivity that, ten years earlier, had so impressed Emma Lazarus. It was because of this that, in her notes, she had seen the old man not only as a lighthouse, but remarkably enough as a bird, a "tall spare figure crowned by the small head carrying out with its birdlike delicacy and poise the aquiline effect of the beaked nose and piercing eyes. Unforgettable eagle eyes, full of smiling wisdom!" Like a bird in a cage—that must have been Emerson's irritated state of mind at staying up half a night to look over a five-act Italian drama, filled with verbal brocades and draperies, with stiff clothes, ruffs and outmoded manners and views that were, for the people of the play, absolutes.

Emerson could not possibly like it—but his relationship to Emma was by that time already so hopelessly confused that he could not tell her. He had been too unjust in the past to be just to her now. Besides, as Ralph L. Rusk has intimated in a letter to the author of this book, no criticism whatsoever of *The Spagnoletto* "would have represented the *real* Emerson, for his memory was by this time so impaired that he was incapable of vigorous thought." Too bad for Emma—for just this very moment would have been the one to show her why her art was here insignificant and a failure. For *The Spagnoletto* was nothing but a miscarriage —though not because it failed as a drama or failed as a historical study.

Only the trained eye of today can see the psychological facts behind this play which make it so conventional. And the compulsion that made it conventional is the real tragedy; what moves us is not at all the tragedy of Ribera the painter and his love for his daughter Maria, which the drama portrays. The work is a choked outcry of the writer herself. An idolized father, a prince of the brush, a famous artist, cannot bear to have his daughter belong to another man. He keeps the girl locked up like a jewel; he would be willing to give her to a king's son, but to none other, none less. This seclusion had to be paid for; life pounded strenuously on the door. It took the form of a king's son in fact—but this Don Juan of Austria could not marry Maria. "Deaf, dumb and blind" because of the upbringing her father gave her, the inexperienced girl falls into the trap and is seduced. After a few weeks her lover casts her aside. But curiously enough, it is not she but her father who is dishonored. All Naples laughs at him and shuns him; he is convinced that he can no longer paint. Before his daughter's eyes he stabs himself, in order that she shall carry the terrible sight with her to all eternity:

> To all dreams
> That haunt thee of past anguish, shall be added
> The vision of this horror!

A truly Dantesque revenge.

The father, the father, nothing but the father. When Emma was fifteen years old she had seen a performance of Donizetti's *Lucia de Lammermoor*; that same night she wrote a poem, "Lucia to Edgardo," with this couplet in it:

> And my stern father sacrificing me
> To long-forgotten feuds of family.

This wholly fanciful notion—that she was sacrificed by a "stern father" and was denied to any other lover—Emma voluptuously cherished her whole life through. It has been overlooked until today that even Ribera's profession, painting, seems a symbol of "paternal activity," for Moses' favorite brother, Jack Lazarus, was a painter by profession. The father-painter alone draws breath in this play. When he speaks it is sometimes (as one verse puts it) as if a vein of fire were flashing in a cloud that silently lies upon Vesuvius. The vital elements in the play are his pride and his collapse, and the mysterious hatred he harbors for Naples' gentry. What could have produced this intensity of hatred? Was it the fact that he was poor and went hungry, that he was nothing but a "little Spaniard" before he became "the Spagnoletto," the famous and sought-after painter?

> No twisted muscle, no contorted limb,
> No agony of flesh, have I yet drawn,
> That owed not its suggestion to some pang
> Of my pride crucified, my spirit racked,
> My entrails gnawed by the blind worm of hate,
> Engendered of oppression. That is past,
> But not forgotten; . . .

This sounds almost like a Jew's speech. Ribera is no Jew. Yet we seem to see the shadows of Shylock and Jessica lurking in the background of the stage; but the comparison with *The Merchant of Venice* is fatal to Emma's drama. Jessica is a real human being; Maria is an utter nonentity; her love scenes are hollow, her seducer no seducer at all; the garden of Ribera's house, which ought to breathe the fragrance of Juliet's garden in the balcony scene, is constructed of cardboard. For Emma had devoted everything to her father, had sacrificed everything to the Moloch of her love for her father. Even to think of another man seemed sinful to her. (When Josephine Lazarus later confessed that she hated the play—for "sinning against our moral and aesthetic instinct"—we can be sure that she did so because Emma, in an almost exhibitionist manner, had revealed her "obsession" with her father's image—something, naturally, that should have been hidden from the eyes of the world.)

But suppose we are mistaken? Suppose that in the depths of Emma's soul there had been a terrible struggle between her father and one of the handsome young men who frequented her house. For, of course, the Lazarus home received many visitors. Sarah and Mary were no longer young. Josephine was rather plain (she and Sarah, after a long life, died spinsters in 1910). Agnes at that time was twenty, and Annie seventeen; Emma, though Annie's senior by a decade, really belonged to the generation of the younger sisters. And among the visiting men were such persons as the sons of Samuel G. Ward, athletic young men, any of whom might easily have been the prototype of Don Juan of Austria. Or had her affections turned to one of the virile members of the Dana clan? Why didn't Emma marry? A rich girl, who was not unattractive. . . . But Moses Lazarus proved the stronger. This fixation upon her father was Emma's real tragedy; yet when *The Spagnoletto* was published in 1876, no contemporary reader perceived this. Her contemporaries sensed only the mysterious failure of a fine talent "that once had held great promise." At the age of twenty-seven Emma Lazarus had experienced nothing but her own verses and the father-god in her family. She was spoiled by family life, hopelessly frustrated—and in the writing of this drama she completely walled herself in. If nothing were to shatter the wall from the outside—some person, thought or mission—Emma Lazarus would be finished as a writer and as a human being.

BOOK TWO: THE GREAT VOCATION

The West refused them, and the East abhorred

15

No ONE HAD FORETOLD at his birth that the Berlin rabbi, Gustav Gottheil, was destined to end his days in America. And, indeed, when he sat in a room of the synagogue on Oranienburger Strasse, learning English, he may well have expected to end his days in Manchester, England. For the Manchester Jewish community had invited him to head the Reform congregation there.

There was a saying that a Jew who spoke German could get along anywhere in the world, and the members of the Manchester congregation were for the most part Anglicized North Germans. Nevertheless, a rabbi who wanted to conduct modern Jewish services in England would have to devote himself seriously to the English language. But with his acquisition of the English language Rabbi Gottheil ran into problems that seemed to expand beyond the limits of Judaism.

There was the matter of America, for example. In America a war was being fought against Negro slavery, that shame of mankind. To hold opinions on slavery and to see in President Lincoln a type of the new Moses was not, in reality, extending one's realm beyond the limits of Judaism, Rabbi Gottheil concluded. And so, in Manchester, Gottheil delivered two magnificent sermons on "Moses versus Slavery." Later he published these sermons in book form.

Slavery was absolutely incompatible with Jewish morality, Gottheil stated and according to the Talmud, ". . . a Hebrew in selling himself into slavery violates the inalienable right which God has in him as an Israelite. This it determines to be the meaning of the text, 'The children of Israel are MY servants'; that is to say, not the servants of servants." Was this Mosaic law meant to apply only to Jews and only to voluntary self-enslavement? To take this view, Rabbi Gottheil concluded, was utterly to mistake the meaning of the "chosen people." Israel was the *teacher* of other nations. As history proceeded, the non-Jews also must profit by what Israel had striven for and won.

A man with such an attitude toward the prime problems of equality and human dignity really belonged in the land of Lincoln. Gottheil's relatives persuaded him to leave his work and his congregation in Manchester and come to New York. He came first upon a visit; then he moved to the New World for good and delivered his sermons in the resplendent Temple Emanu-El, on the corner of Fifth Avenue and Forty-third Street.

The members of this congregation appeared to be almost entirely composed of wealthy Jews. New York had moved uptown and Fifth Avenue had become the Champs Elysées of the city. West Fourteenth Street was now no longer the farthest outpost of the "aristocrats." And the synagogue itself, whose architect was Henry Fernbach, considerably influenced this shift in the Jewish population. The exterior of the temple indicated at a glance how much it must have cost. Never before had Rabbi Gottheil preached in such elegant surroundings. It seemed to be a difficult task to remind these worshippers of the sufferings of their forefathers, for the children's children whom fortune has always smiled upon easily forget. Rabbi Gustav Gottheil observed this forgetfulness in the homes of the rich where he gave private instruction. Among others, was the home of the Lazarus family. These people were certainly prosperous—but did that make them good Jews?

The rabbi was naturally most interested in the gifted young girl, Emma, who was publishing some of her poems in the *Jewish Messenger*. He thought of her as one of the "good" Jews; he had every reason to think so. For he had read her deeply felt poem, "In the Jewish Synagogue at Newport," which she had written at the age of nineteen.

> Here, where the noises of the busy town,
>   The ocean's plunge and roar can enter not,
> We stand and gaze around with tearful awe,
>   And muse upon the consecrated spot.
>   . . . .
> What prayers were in this temple offered up,
>   Wrung from sad hearts that knew no joy on earth,
> By these lone exiles of a thousand years,
>   From the fair sunrise land that gave them birth!
>   . . . .
> Again we see the patriarch with his flocks,
>   The purple seas, the hot blue sky o'erhead,
> The slaves of Egypt,—omens, mysteries,—
>   Dark fleeing hosts by flaming angels led.
>   . . . .
> The pride of luxury's barbaric pomp,
>   In the rich court of royal Solomon—
> Alas! we wake: one scene alone remains,—
>   The exiles by the streams of Babylon.
>
> Our softened voices send us back again
>   But mournful echoes through the empty hall;
> Our footsteps have a strange, unnatural sound,
>   And with unwonted gentleness they fall.
>   . . . .

The funeral and the marriage, now, alas!
  We know not which is sadder to recall;
For youth and happiness have followed age,
  And green grass lieth gently over all.

Nathless the sacred shrine is holy yet,
  With its lone floors where reverent feet once trod.
Take off your shoes as by the burning bush,
  Before the mystery of death and God.

The abandoned synagogue at Newport was certainly a "consecrated spot" for all the Jews in America. For there, in the heart of the Puritan colony of Rhode Island, the oldest Jewish congregation had been established around 1660; Sephardic Jews from Brazil had mingled here with the Ashkenazic Jews from Central and Eastern Europe. This congregation had been larger and more illustrious than that of New York, but with the passage of time it had vanished from history.

The poem was beautiful. Rabbi Gottheil was at this time engaged in work on a new prayer book for his congregation, a prayer book in which Jewish ritual would draw upon the richness of the English language. There was urgent need of such a revision, for the only prayer book had long since been outmoded. Its English was poor and its hymns mediocre in quality and in style. The translations from the Hebrew and the German had been made by men who were better German than English scholars. If the younger generation was to be attracted to the temple, a radical change was needed. Emma Lazarus seemed to Gottheil the ideal person to whom to turn for assistance in his task.

To his surprise she replied that she would not be able to write to order. "I will gladly assist you as far as I can; but that will not be much. I shall always be loyal to my race, but I feel no religious fervor in my soul. . . ."

The rabbi was disturbed. Didn't the girl understand the ties of destiny that linked the ancient people and its religion? . . . In reality, Emma's reply was simply "Emersonian." For the sage of Concord too had one day given up being a Protestant preacher, that is to say, had ceased to give adherence to one religion alone. Emma agreed with Emerson, and with Felix Adler, founder of the Society for Ethical Culture, that the essence of religion appeared to be ethics—and ethics was the monopoly of no one faith. There was, however, another element in the situation which the rabbi did not understand. Emma was a romantic, and romantics love "ruins." They absorb life out of the past; they literally need death that they may imagine life. Their poesy is "tearful, awing and musing." "Something to Weep Over" is the title of a poem Emma wrote at thirteen. When in 1877 Emma's uncle-in-law, Rabbi Jacques I. Lyons, died, she wrote him a moving farewell:

For there is mourning now in Israel.
The crown, the garland of the branching tree
Is plucked . . . Ripe of years was he,
The priest, the good old man who wrought so well
Upon his chosen glebe. . . .

But this really was less concerned with the Jewish rabbi than with the old romantic "awe of mortality." And Emma's genuine emotion in the synagogue at Newport had been inspired by thoughts of death rather than of the Jews. She might have dedicated to any other vanished community her elegiac lines about "the funeral and the marriage, we know not which is sadder to recall." For, at that time, nurtured chiefly on Byron, she was an elegiac poet seemingly under all circumstances. But when, on account of the Newport elegy, a request came to her to do a service for her coreligionists, she shrank back. She had no desire, at that time, to figure in a prayer book. The fact that, as early as 1879, she had published some very beautiful translations (also in the *Jewish Messenger*) of Ibn Gabirol, Ibn Ezra and Halevi, the great Jewish singers of medieval Spain, must not be given too much weight. Apparently she had done these translations in a spirit no different from that in which she had translated verses of Goethe, Musset, Heine and Hugo. Although there have been more than a few attempts to trace Emma Lazarus' "conversion" to religious Judaism much farther back than the August of 1881, all such attempts were unavailing. Indeed, since Richard Gottheil's publication in 1936 of Emma's letters to his father, Gustav Gottheil, we must not imagine the bond uniting her to Judaism before the summer of 1881 any stronger than those uniting her to other ancient cultures, such as the Greek, the Italian, or the German.

Some of these astonishing letters to Rabbi Gottheil express a reluctance to have anything to do with things religious. Almost all of them have a curious evasiveness and show a real anxiety about touching too strongly on Jewish subjects. It is almost as if the freethinking part of Emma balked at the thought of becoming a "Jewish writer."

Thus, when the rabbi reminded her in a letter of the translations she had made some years earlier, she answered on June 29, 1881: "I have no recollection of having translated any Hymns for you"! And when the puzzled rabbi then sent her the originals on July 27, 1881, she managed still to write: "I have read over the translations without a gleam of recognition. I do not remember a single line nor a single circumstance connected with them and if it were not that I saw my own handwriting, I could not believe that they were my work. . . ."

This is a bit strong. Even if we allow for a certain amount of playfulness and coquetry here (qualities otherwise totally lacking in her personal relations with the other sex but occasionally evident in her literary letters), nevertheless these lines call for only one conclusion. Since, short of amnesia, it was impossible for a writer as painstaking and responsible as she was to forget lines she herself had carefully composed, we must conclude that she did not care at that time to be mixed up with what she must have thought so sectarian an undertaking as a Jewish prayer book.

Rabbi Gottheil shrugged his shoulders. As so often in his life, he had to fall back on a favorite expression of his: "*Deo favente,* I'll try again." But other forces than this single rabbi would have to be brought to bear upon Emma Lazarus before she would write down the words: "It is principally my own ignorance that has given me my heretical opinions in regard to the Jewish genius." It was the August of 1881 that was destined to change her whole life.

16

On March 13, 1881, bombs thrown by Nihilists destroyed the Czar of Russia, Alexander II. It was a tragic day for the whole world.

To be sure, the man who fell upon the snow, both legs torn off, able only to whisper a last "Help me, brother" to another victim lying near him, was no longer the intrepid humanitarian he had been thirty years earlier. Alexander was no longer the enemy of ecclesiastical reaction and the young emperor who had abolished serfdom and the death sentence. The wine of his life had turned sour from the time a corrupt bureaucracy forced him, the "Czar of Liberation," to follow the path of all the past czars—to decide that the people were not yet mature enough to be trusted.

Now he had received his deathblow at the hands of the

extremists. His son, Alexander III, who ascended the throne next day, naturally blamed the disaster on the recent reforms. Before two weeks had passed all Russia was whispering that the Jews were to blame for the death of the great Czar.

There had been no Jews at all in Russia until little more than a hundred years before. The grand dukes and czars had kept the people of Israel out of the Empire and had boasted that "within the borders of the Holy Russian Empire there lives no circumcised dog." But in 1772 this state of affairs suddenly changed. In the first partition of Poland millions of Polish Jews became Russian subjects. This happened virtually overnight. Catherine the Great, motivated by the ideas of the Enlightenment, then issued an edict: "Religious liberty and inviolability of property are hereby granted to all subjects of Russia and certainly to the Jews also; for the humanitarian principles of Her Majesty do not permit the exclusion of the Jews alone from the favors shown to all, so long as they, like faithful subjects, continue to employ themselves as hitherto in commerce and handicrafts, each according to his vocation."

On paper this ukase looked splendid; in practice the Russian state, from the noble governors down to the pettiest officials, labored to prevent its realization. Not only were the Polish Jews not permitted to enter old Russia, but from decade to decade they were gradually deprived of the rights they had enjoyed under Polish rule. The only ruler who had taken a resolute stand against total nullification of the rights of his Jewish subjects had been Alexander II. And it was this ruler whom the Jews were accused of having murdered!

The Nihilist conspiracy drew upon all strata of the Russian nation. It was therefore not surprising that Rosa Helfmann and Aaron Zundelevitch were Jews. It was sheer chance that two of the terrorists were Jews—but that was the sum of Jewish complicity in the conspiracy. The majority of the Jews in western Russia were horrified by the news of Alexander's assassination. They shared the view of Lord Beaconsfield, the British Prime Minister, that the murdered Czar had been "the most gentle prince that ever ruled Russia."

With a speed and organization that were astonishing for Russian conditions, the first pogroms began, six weeks after the assassination of the Czar. On April 27, 1881, rioting flared up in Elisavetgrad, and from May 8 to May 11 the mob devastated the Jewish quarter of Kiev. Police and soldiers stood by and did not lift a hand to prevent the violence. The governor general of Kiev, Drenteln, a Baltic baron, gave a bland answer to a Jewish delegation: "I cannot endanger the lives of my soldiers for the sake of a few Jews." (According to English correspondents he expressed himself in even more shameless terms.) Foreigners observed that each time rioting started at some place, there was present in the vicinity a band of young men, strangers, well dressed and always provided with ample funds which they freely dispensed on treating the populace to drink. Everything had been organized from above. For half a year the pogrom moved methodically through one hundred and fifty small towns. Almost all Jewish property was smashed or stolen, great numbers of men, women and children were killed, injured or driven away.

In order to save face before the outside world, Alexander III and his government promised an official "settlement of the Jewish question." This "settlement" turned out to be the notorious May Laws of 1882. It was well known that the Russian Jews lived under fearfully crowded conditions where they literally stumbled over one another's feet in fifteen western provinces. Now—under the hypocritical pretext of desiring to shield the Jews from the hatred of the peasants—the May Laws established new reservations within the older ones; Jews were expressly forbidden to live outside of town and city. Not only were the Jews shut off physically from the open country, but all mortgages and leases held by Jews on landed estates were canceled. This was attacking the tree at its root. To be totally cut off from the land, from trade with peasants and non-Jews, was in an agrarian country like Russia in the long run a direr fate than the pogroms. What had apparently been a series of spontaneous acts of wanton violence was now legally sanctioned. Up to now a corrupt state had permitted individual citizens to purchase their "rights" by large and small bribes. When broad masses of the Jewish community realized that in the future this would no longer be possible, they drew the logical conclusion.

And so hundreds of thousands of refugees flowed toward the borders of Russia and on to other countries, to the ports, to the sea.

17

In early August of 1881 the first human cargo from Russia arrived in New York and was unloaded at Wards Island in upper Manhattan, far from the noise and bustle of the port. Barracks had been set up, committees were functioning to provide food for the refugees and to take care of the legal problems of their entry.

Harold Frederic later wrote a classic description of the first arrivals among the Russian Jews who had crossed the Russian border into Germany. "Pathetic stories were told me in Berlin of the terror and ignorance of the earlier refugees, who came shortly after the fierce Passover persecutions. The committee had arranged with the railroad authorities for the use of a disused tunnel in which to feed and examine the exiles during their halt at Ruhleben. The panic-stricken wretches could with difficulty be brought to comprehend that at last they were among friends. They were afraid to eat the food set before them for fear it was not *kosher*; they fought against giving up their tickets, to be changed for others; especially were they terrified at being compelled to enter the tunnel, which seemed to them like another Russian prison. Some were found who, at the sight of this, suspected that they had been brought to Siberia instead of Germany. One woman, rather than go into the tunnel, snatched up her two babes, and, screaming as she ran, leaped upon the track before the advancing train, and was rescued at great risk and by a veritable hair's breadth. The people who come now are more tranquil, but still difficult to manage often enough."

For the first time Emma saw persecuted people. "What does it mean, persecuted?" she had, as a child, innocently asked her father. Now her own eyes provided her with the answer. Gaunt men and women, many in black caftan costumes so worn that the cloth shimmered with reddish or greenish hues. A kindly Berlin committee had provided some of them, on their passage through Germany, with European dress. It had been well meant but the clothes were often ill chosen, a trembling housewife would be wearing a bird-of-paradise hat or a Nile-green blouse that might have created a stir in the Berlin *Tiergartenviertel*. Some of the men wore dandyish pointed shoes or dashing straw hats; but the wretched bundles in which all carried their belongings told the indubitable truth.

The poor and the well-to-do, those who had never possessed anything and those who had had to leave everything behind them, were united in their common suffering. Their faces showed the ravages of grief, their eyes were red from wakeful nights and tears. And their beards! Those were beards such as Emma knew only from old paintings; they were the beards of the prophets, such as Rembrandt had painted. Terror had marked these faces like a disfiguration, but a certain dignity appeared in them nevertheless, like a light in an ugly hovel.

All occupations were represented: the peddler who spoke a strange German mingled with scraps of Hebrew and Russian; the big merchant, the engineer, the former landowner, the university professor, the pawnbroker, the money-changer, the tavern keeper, the doctor, the lawyer—and all their wives. What a motley company! This was the host of the Exodus who had once fled from Egypt to Canaan; these were the Spanish Jews who had sought shelter in Turkey, and the German Jews of the Middle Ages who had fled from pyres to Eastern Europe. And these, the great-great-grandchildren of those people, were now knocking on the doors of America.

The purely visual experience swiftly pierced to Emma's heart. "A conversion cannot be painted," a great French Jesuit father had said, a man who in his life insisted upon the need for conversions. Painting can fix but a single moment, and conversion is a subject outside of its sphere. For the suddenness is an illusion, and the accounts of conversions that take place "all of a sudden" must be fictional.

But life abounds in the fictional. Emma Lazarus had come as a lady among other ladies, as a member of a welfare committee (because she was rich), and, too, out of a certain curiosity. When she returned home from her visit to Wards Island she could not sleep. And during the sleepless nights that followed, a new, a different poet was born within her. The author of the *Songs of a Semite* emerged, and spoke with a powerful voice to which, before long, thousands would listen.

18

When the first news of the assassination of Czar Alexander II reached New York on March 13, 1881, in a somewhat "Byronian temper" Emma had sat down to write a poem, "Sic Semper Liberatoribus!" But the title, which echoed Booth's cry of "Sic semper tyrannis!" as he slew Lincoln, was ill-chosen and the poem itself not too well written. What it chiefly expressed was a woman's loathing of *all* bloodshed (and this is probably the reason why Josephine took this weak poem into the first edition [1889] of Emma's collected works). And then, moreover (we cannot keep from mentioning this!), it has for its subject the murder of a "poor old man"—that father figure we have come upon so often before.

Well, it is done! A most heroic plan,
Which after myriad plots succeeds at last
In robbing of his life one poor old man,
Whose sole offense—his birthright—has but passed
To fresher blood, with younger strength recast.
What men are these, who, clamoring to be free,
Would bestialize the world to what they be?

Yet surely she was carrying matters rather far when she went on to write:

Whose sons are they who made that snow-wreathed head
Their frenzy's target? In their Russian veins,
What alien current urged on to smite him dead
Whose word has loosed a million Russian chains?
What brutes were they for whom such speechless pains,
So royally endured, no human thrill
Awoke, in hearts drunk with the lust to kill?

Not brutes! No tiger of the wilderness,
No jackal of the jungle, bears such brand
As man's black heart, who shrinks not to confess
The desperate deed of his deliberate hand.
Our kind, our kin, have done this thing. We stand
Bowed earthward, red with shame, to see such wrong
Prorogue Love's cause and Truth's—God knows how long!

From a purely humane point of view, all this was entirely correct—and at the same time it was entirely false. For history, which is written for all men, is more important than the single individual, lamentable as this fact is to a real poet. Alexander, the humanitarian, the "liberator of the peasants," came one hundred years too late into the world. That was so to speak his historic guilt. His reforms, which were too mild and whose intent, moreover, the Russian bureaucracy frustrated, were unable to save Russia. The "tiger" of the Revolution, the Nihilists, that Emma vilified in this poem—what was that jungle, really, in which it had been born? Was it not that same Russia which Nekrasov and Alexander Herzen had called a prison? And did not Sophie Perovskaya's violent deed, which Alexander II fell victim to, like all such deeds show all the characteristics of a typical prison outbreak?

Eight weeks after, Emma, most laboriously, had written her poem. And *now* what broke out of the jungle, leaping with deadly fangs at the throats of innocent Jews, was no longer the "tiger" of the Revolution. It was, as everyone well knew, the opposed forces, the "Holy Terror" of the Right—although Alexander III, with a show of concern, had dared mumble to Baron Guenzberg (who had to be reckoned with because of his family connections abroad) that "these anti-Jewish riots are the work of the Nihilists."

Emma, as we know, was easily stirred. A dispatch in a

New York newspaper could send a flood of feelings racing through her. Yet what she saw on Wards Island—the pitiful mass of a humanity brought low, the innocent misery of refugees—made a new person and poet out of her.

19

Now poems thronged to her mind. But they were not really what she had formerly considered to be poetry. They were fanfares and appeals. All that she had ever learned about love of justice, philosophy and poetics (until now these things had existed within her mind in a disconnected and inorganic association) was now synthesized into an act of character. Her poems were redder, fiercer than the sky over Russia when it flamed with the glare of burning Jewish villages. There was the "Crowing of the Red Cock":

> Across the Eastern sky has glowed
>   The flicker of a blood-red dawn,
> Once more the clarion cock has crowed,
>   Once more the sword of Christ is drawn.
> A million burning rooftrees light
> The world-wide path of Israel's flight.
>
> Where is the Hebrew's fatherland?
>   The folk of Christ is sore bested;
> The son of Man is bruised and banned,
>   Nor finds whereon to lay his head.
> His cup is gall, his meat is tears,
> His passion lasts a thousand years.
>
> Each crime that wakes in man the beast,
>   Is visited upon his kind.
> The lust of mobs, the greed of priest,
>   The tyranny of kings, combined
> To root his seed from earth again,
> His record is one cry of pain.

When the long roll of Christian guilt
    Against his sires and kin is known,
The flood of tears, the life-blood spilt,
    The agony of ages shown,
What oceans can the stain remove,
From Christian law and Christian love?

Nay, close the book; not now, not here,
    The hideous tale of sin narrate,
Reechoing in the martyr's ear,
    Even he might nurse revengeful hate,
Even he might turn in wrath sublime,
With blood for blood and crime for crime.

Coward? Not he, who faces death,
    Who singly against worlds has fought,
For what? A name he may not breathe,
    For liberty of prayer and thought.
The angry sword he will not whet,
His nobler task is—to forget.

    The Jewish cause is a strange one. It always has two dimensions. In part it is the oldest cause in the world and has the cast of classic immobility; it is draped in priestly garments and speaks in parables that are out of date. And on the other hand it is the most disturbing and the most modern of all topics. It has an ever variable present-day significance; it has all the contemporaneity of a newspaper headline.

    Emma Lazarus with her sentimental, historical bent had always been attracted by the first dimension of Judaism. She was persuaded that she had no talent for "getting excited about the newspapers." But she underwent a total reversal on this score. In 1881 and 1882 the day's news became a prime intellectual stimulus for her. One day she saw the people on Wards Island, the next she read about acts of incendiarism—and she turned almost immediately to writing ballads.

By nature she was an elegiac poet. For this reason the ballad form was something she had no experience of. A ballad does not tell a story; it enacts and portrays; it is almost a dramatic poem. Perhaps the "influence" on Emma's ballads was that fine poem of Lord Byron's, "The Destruction of Sennacherib":

> The Assyrian came down like the wolf on the fold,
> And his cohorts were gleaming in purple and gold;
> And the sheen of their spears was like stars on the sea,
> When the blue wave rolls nightly on deep Galilee.

The poem is one of the *Hebrew Melodies*, which Byron had written in 1815. Distinguished in form, they reflect something of the Anglo-Protestant appreciation of the Old Testament, an appreciation that speaks in mightier tones in Handel's music. In one passage the sympathy for the language and thought of the Hebrew Bible reaches a peak of perception into the tragedy of the Jews:

> The wild-dove hath her nest, the fox his cave,
> Mankind their country—Israel but the grave!

Byron, remarkably enough, disliked the poems and had been on the point of tossing them into the fire. It was only after the Jewish composer Nathan had upbraided him for this that he hesitantly decided to publish them. Probably Byron himself knew that they lacked the essential force of "Byronic indignation." For this very reason Emma could learn little from these poems. In the *Songs of a Semite* the indignation was her own. The poems arose out of the historical situation and Emma's apprehension of what it meant in human terms.

It is odd that for the writing of these aggressive poems she could learn nothing from Heine either. For Heine was one of her lifelong interests. Not only did she translate him, but she could turn out imitations of Heine with deceptive skill. To her translation of his famous ballad, "Donna Clara," with its sardonic surprise ending—

> Then the knight with gentle laughter,
>   Kissed the fingers of his Donna,
> Kissed her lips and kissed her forehead,
>   And at last these words he uttered:
>
> "I, Senora, your beloved,
>   Am the son of the respected,
> Worthy, erudite Grand Rabbi
>   Israel of Saragossa!"

—she appended two ballads of her own, "Don Pedrillo" and "Fra Pedro," which caused admirers of Heine to ask: "Where are the German originals?"

But in the hour of her conversion to Judaism Heine could scarcely serve Emma as an example. For Heine, the great scoffer, had all too often also scoffed at the Jews. A poem such as his "Prinzessin Sabbat," in which the holiest thoughts were drowned in an orgiastic revel of eating and drinking, could be no help whatsoever at a time of fearful decision for Israel; it could not aid Emma Lazarus when she raised "The Banner of the Jew."

> Wake, Israel, wake! Recall to-day
>   The glorious Maccabean rage,
> The sire heroic, hoary-gray,
>   His five-fold lion-lineage:
> The Wise, the Elect, the Help-of-God,
>   The Burst-of-Spring, the Avenging Rod.

From Mizpeh's mountain-ridge they saw
    Jerusalem's empty streets, her shrine
Laid waste where Greeks profaned the Law,
    With idol and with pagan sign.
Mourners in tattered black were there,
    With ashes sprinkled on their hair.

Then from the stony peak there rang
    A blast to ope the graves: down poured
The Maccabean clan, who sang
    Their battle-anthem to the Lord.
Five heroes lead, and following, see
    Ten thousand rush to victory!

Oh for Jerusalem's trumpet now,
    To blow a blast of shattering power,
To wake the sleepers high and low,
    And rouse them to the urgent hour!
No hand for vengeance—but to save,
    A million naked swords should wave.

Oh deem not dead that martial fire,
    Say not the mystic flame is spent!
With Moses' law and David's lyre,
    Your ancient strength remains unbent.
Let but an Ezra rise anew,
    To lift the *Banner of the Jew*!

A rag, a mock at first—erelong,
    When men have bled and women wept,
To guard its precious folds from wrong,
    Even they who shrank, even they who slept,
Shall leap to bless it, and to save.
    Strike! for the brave revere the brave!

What a remarkable transformation this is! This poem, of **course**, could have been written only by a lover of the historical, by an imagination aroused by the *mythus* of the Maccabees; but the effect of the poem was strictly contemporaneous. Read at a Jewish meeting, recited at a Jewish school, it set hearts on fire. And such words were found and framed by a woman who only yesterday had been little more than a shy daughter, "one in love with solitude and song"; by a timorous person who had only recently confessed to her friend Stedman that she had accomplished nothing "to stir or awake"; who had written such repining verses as these:

> Late-born and woman-souled I dare not hope,
> The freshness of the elder lays, the might
> Of manly, modern passion shall alight
> Upon my Muse's lips, nor may I cope
> (Who veiled and screened by womanhood must grope)
> With the world's strong-armed warriors and recite
> The dangers, wounds and triumphs of the fight;

It is as if a poor Ruth, a gleaner of the corn, had overnight become a Deborah who had drunk of the wine of victory and could move, dancing, at the head of the people. . . . And along with these songs of struggle we find the quiet summing-up in the poem "Gifts," in which Emma Lazarus declared her philosophy of history.

> "O World-God, give me Wealth!" the Egyptian cried.
> His prayer was granted. High as Heaven, behold
> Palace and Pyramid; the brimming tide
> Of lavish Nile washed all his land with gold.
> Armies of slaves toiled ant-wise at his feet,
> World-circling traffic roared through mart and street,
> His priests were gods, his spice-balmed kings enshrined,
> Set death at naught in rock-ribbed charnels deep.
> Seek Pharaoh's race to-day and ye shall find
> Rust and the moth, silence and dusty sleep.

Egyptian civilization is followed by the Hellenic age:

"O World-God, give me Beauty!" cried the Greek.
His prayer was granted. All the earth became
Plastic and vocal to his sense; each peak,
Each grove, each stream, quick with Promethean flame,
Peopled the world with imaged grace and light.
The lyre was his, and his the breathing might
Of the immortal marble, his the play
Of diamond-pointed thought and golden tongue.
Go seek the sun-shine race, ye find to-day
A broken column and a lute unstrung.

Then the Roman occupies the stage:

"O World-God, give me Power!" the Roman cried.
His prayer was granted. The vast world was chained
A captive to the chariot of his pride.
The blood of myriad provinces was drained
To feed that fierce, insatiable red heart.
Invulnerably bulwarked every part
With serried legions and with close-meshed code,
Within, the burrowing worm had gnawed its home,
A roofless ruin stands where once abode
The imperial race of everlasting Rome.

But what was the Hebrew's prayer?

"O Godhead, give me Truth!" the Hebrew cried.
His prayer was granted; he became the slave
Of the Idea, a pilgrim far and wide,
Cursed, hated, spurned and scourged with none to save.
The Pharaohs knew him, and when Greece beheld,
His wisdom wore the hoary crown of Eld.
Beauty he hath forsworn, and wealth and power.
Seek him to-day, and find in every land.

No fire consumes him, neither floods devour;
Immortal through the lamp within his hand.

20

Some have said of Emma Lazarus that "she was no longer content to sing of long vanished crusaders, but herself became a crusader." This does not quite do justice to the historical consciousness that informs her poems (as well as the polemics she was shortly to write). Her historical leanings always remained with her and gave depth to her writings, whether poetical or polemical, without detracting in the least from their force.

Not too long after the Russian pogroms she published a poem in the *American Hebrew* that one might call a *disputatio theologica*. This disputation took place in Old Spain, a country that had once been of great importance to the Sephardic Lazarus family. Emma was aware (nor was she the only one, of course) of the striking resemblance between what had taken place in Old Spain and what was now going on in Russia. She knew, too, that in both instances there were ideological factors as well as greed behind the persecution of the Jews. In a manner she was bearding the lion in his own den when she entitled her poem "An Epistle from Joshua Ibn Vives of Allorqui to His Former Master, Solomon Levi-Paul, de Santa-Maria, Bishop of Cartagena, Chancellor of Castile."

Who was the baptized Jew to whom this loyal Jew addressed this epistle? Emma Lazarus found the sources for her poem and the characters of the two men in Volume VIII of Heinrich Graetz' *History of the Jews:* "Among the Jews baptized in 1391, no other wrought as much harm to his race as the Rabbi Solomon Levi of Burgos, known to Christians as Paulus Burgensis or de Santa Maria . . .

who rose to very high ecclesiastical and political rank. . . . He had no philosophical culture; on the contrary, as a Jew, he had been extremely devout, observing scrupulously all the rites, and regarded as a pillar of Judaism in his own circle. . . . Possessed by ambition and vanity, the synagogue where he had passed a short time in giving and receiving instruction, appeared to him too narrow and restricted a sphere. He longed for a bustling activity, aimed at a position at court, in whatever capacity, began to live on a grand scale, maintained a sumptuous equipage, a spirited team, and a numerous retinue of servants. As his affairs brought him into daily contact with Christians and entangled him in religious discussions, he studied ecclesiastical literature in order to display his erudition. The bloody massacre of 1391 robbed him of all hope of reaching eminence as a Jew, in his fortieth year, and he abruptly resolved to be baptized. The lofty degree of dignity which he afterwards attained in Church and State, may even then have floated alluringly before his mind . . . the convert gave out that . . . the . . . writings of . . . Aquinas [had] taken hold of his inmost convictions. The Jews, however, mistrusted his credulity and knowing him well, they ascribed this step to his ambition and his thirst for fame. His family, consisting of a wife and son, renounced him when he changed his faith. . . . The campaign against the malignity of Paul the Santa Maria was opened by a young man who had formerly sat at his feet, Joshua ben Joseph Ibn Vives, from the town of Lorca or Allorqui, a physician and Arabic scholar. In an epistle written in a tone of humility as from a docile pupil to a revered master, he deals his apostate teacher heavy blows. . . ." And it is these blows which one can hear resound in Emma's poem. Availing herself of the stanza Byron had used in his *Don Juan*, the poet has Joshua Ibn Vives write thus:

Where are the signs fulfilled whereby all men
   Should know the Christ? Where is the wide-winged peace
Shielding the lamb within the lion's den?
   The freedom broadening with the wars that cease?
Do foes clasp hands in brotherhood again?
   Where is the promised garden of increase,
When like a rose the wilderness should bloom?
Earth is a battlefield and Spain a tomb.

Our God of Sabaoth is an awful God
   Of lightnings and of vengeance,—Christians say.
Earth trembled, nations perished at his nod;
   His law has yielded to a milder sway.
Theirs is the God of Love whose feet have trod
   Our common earth—draw near to him and pray,
Meek-faced, dove-eyed, pure-browed, the Lord of life,
Know him and kneel, else at your throat the knife!

This is the God of Love, whose altars reek
   With human blood, who teaches men to hate;
Torture past words, or sins we may not speak
   Wrought by his priests behind the convent-grate.
Are his priests false? or are his doctrines weak
   That none obeys him? State at war with state,
Church against church—yea, Pope at feud with Pope
In these tossed seas what anchorage for hope?

Not only for the sheep without the fold,
   Is the knife whetted, who refuse to share
Blessings the shepherd wise doth not withhold
   Even from the least among his flock—but there
Midmost the pale, dissensions manifold,
   Lamb flaying lamb, fierce sheep that rend and tear.
Master, if thou to thy pride's goal should come,
Where wouldst thou throne—at Avignon or Rome?

I handle burning questions, good my Lord,
   Such as may kindle fagots, well I wis.
Your Gospel not denies our older Word,
   But in a way completes and betters this.
The Law of Love shall supersede the sword,
   So runs the promise, but the facts I miss.
Already needs this wretched generation,
A voice divine—a new, third revelation.

At that time Christianity had fallen on evil days, with a creature of the French living as Pope at Avignon, and another Pope seated on the throne in Rome. Emma's Joshua Ibn Vives alludes to this in his diatribe, masterfully compounded both of genuine devotion and proud irony:

Two Popes and their adherents fulminate
   Ban against ban, and to the nether hell
Condemn each other, while the nations wait
   Their Christ to thunder forth from Heaven, and tell
Who is his rightful Vicar, reinstate
   His throne, the hideous discord to dispel.
Where shall I seek, master, while such things be,
Celestial truth, revealed certainty?

Not miracles I doubt, for how dare man,
   Chief miracle of life's mystery, say *he knows*?
How may he closely secret causes scan,
   Who learns not whence he comes nor where he goes?
Like one who walks in sleep a doubtful span
   He gropes through all his days, till Death unclose
His cheated eyes and in one blinding gleam,
Wakes, to discern the substance from the dream.

I say not therefore I deny the birth,
   The Virgin's motherhood, the resurrection,
Who know not how mine own soul came to earth,
   Nor what shall follow death. Man's imperfection

May bound not even in thought the height and girth
  Of God's Omnipotence; neath his direction
We may approach his essence, but that He
  Should dwarf Himself to us—it cannot be!

The God who balances the clouds, who spread
  The sky above us like a molten glass,
The God who shut the sea with doors, who laid
  The corner-stone of earth, who caused the grass
Spring forth upon the wilderness, and made
  The darkness scatter and the night to pass—
That He should clothe Himself with flesh, and move
Midst worms a worm—this, sun, moon, stars disprove.

Help me, O thou who wast my boyhood's guide,
  I bend my exile-weary feet to thee,
Teach me the indivisible to divide,
  Show me how three are one and One is three!
How Christ to save all men was crucified,
  Yet I and mine are damned eternally.
Instruct me, Sage, why Virtue starves alone,
While falsehood step by step ascends the throne.

21

But no poem alone, though it be the most eloquent, nor theological wisdom, nor the wit of sages could help that little band of two hundred and fifty Jews on Wards Island. If this wave of persecution and banishment continued to roll over Russia, there might one day be a good two hundred and fifty thousand of them. The Jews of the East had begun to move—this was a political fact that had not only causes, but also consequences. These consequences had to be faced, and that again was a matter of politics.

With politics Emma Lazarus had never had any dealings. Politics was filth; politics was connected with elections, scandals, bribery and ugly lust for power. "Every actual State is corrupt," Emerson, her great teacher, had written, and he had gone on to say that the word *politic* "now for ages has signified *cunning*." Why should a person like herself be interested in something that was the antithesis of art, kindness, humanity, nobility?

But she had to be. The hour had struck. And she began to look about her to see what this exodus of Jews from Russia had to do with world politics. What position were the great powers taking on it? And what levers must be moved in order to improve the lot of the refugees and of those who remained in Russia?

There was, first of all, Russia's great neighbor. One would think that Germany was the natural champion of the menaced Jews. Germany should have been the executor of the humanistic heritage of Moses Mendelssohn, Lessing and Schiller. Yet these ideas were held only at the upper pinnacles of German culture. The German petty bourgeois, hating and fearing Jewish diligence, rather felt spitefully elated when the smell of blood and burning wafted across the borders. And Emma Lazarus understood this; she had read her favorite poet, Heine, too well to hope for much relief from Germany.

But France, she thought, was different. France, it was true, had seen anti-Semitic agitation in the forties. Yet the Alliance Israélite Universelle, which was collecting money for the Russian refugees, was able to count upon the sympathy of non-Jewish Frenchmen. Nor had public opinion in France forgotten the Crimean War against Russia. To Frenchmen, czarism was a horror, and this feeling had long precedent. After all, it was in the icy wastes of Russia that Napoleon's army had disintegrated in 1812. And ten years earlier, when Bismarck's soldiers had marched into Paris—had not the Prussian known that his rear was covered by Russia? The German-speaking aristocrats of Russia's Baltic provinces who had long furnished Russia with generals and governors, kept up close ties with their Berlin cousins. The Russians had rejoiced at the defeat of the French. . . . And for these reasons not a week passed without sharp caricatures in Parisian newspapers of the vodka bottle and the knout, of bribery and the Orthodox priests—the symbols of Russia.

But France was a powerless country. A more significant factor was the hatred for Russia in London. In 1878 when the Russian bureaucracy forced the hesitant Czar to declare war on Turkey, England instantly felt her own interests threatened. The Pan-Slavic movement, the idea of the brotherhood of all the Slavic peoples—and that Russia as the eldest brother had to look after the well-being of all Slavs—assailed the position of the British Empire in the Mediterranean. Already Russian armies were entering upon the soil of Bulgaria. If the Russians won Constantinople, England's shipping route to India would be threatened. Moreover, British India was also menaced via the land route: a Russian military mission was stirring up trouble in Afghanistan. Another Anglo-Russian war seemed almost inevitable; the British fleet was hastily sent to the Dardanelles to provide fighting Turkey with "diplomatic" support. All that prevented a world war at that time was the fact that Germany did not want war and succeeded in mediating between England and the Czar at the Congress of Berlin.

Newspapers . . . maps . . . Russia, Germany, France, England . . . the contradictory movements, the complexity and interdependence—that was world politics. And the Jewish question was interwoven with world politics, as

Emma was astonished to discover. Wherever Israel bled, a part of the world always bled as well.

Up until recently the British Empire had had for Prime Minister a Jew. The Earl of Beaconsfield was by birth Benjamin Disraeli. Naturally, Disraeli would have carried through as firm a policy toward Russia if he had not been a Jew. Nevertheless, it was a piece of great good fortune for the British Jews, who were drawing up manifestoes and holding mass meetings to protest the persecution of their coreligionists in Russia, that they were assured of having all England on their side. The man on the street might mean India when he shouted, "Down with Russia!" but the British Jews also thought of Odessa, Balta, Elisavetgrad and the blood of their brother Jews. Russia was the common enemy.

Since the beginning of the nineteenth century English had become the principal international language. French had been losing ground since the defeat of Napoleon; German was not yet thought of as an international language. It was therefore quite natural that whatever was thought and printed in London swiftly circulated around the globe and was discussed and often given credence in Calcutta, Sidney, Capetown and the Honduras. And, of course, in New York. When a protest meeting against czarism was organized in London at which spokesmen for public opinion supported the cause of the persecuted Jews, a corresponding protest meeting would often be held the same day in New York, or at most a few weeks later.

22

On Wednesday, February 1, 1882, a mass meeting was held in Chittering Hall in New York. There was an unusual amount of bustle. When Emma Lazarus looked up at the platform where sat the committee who had called the meeting, she recognized the faces of the foremost citizens of the American nation.

This "meeting of the citizens of New York without distinction of creed . . . for the purpose of expressing their sympathy with the persecuted Hebrews in the Russian Empire" had been convoked by seventy-five non-Jewish citizens. At their head stood Ulysses S. Grant, the man who had twice been elected President of the United States. Although he had long since laid aside his general's uniform, the people still saw him as the great hero of the Civil War. He was a strong, silent man who retired into his beard and seldom wasted words. Today, too, he would have little part in the speaking; he was leaving the chief burden of oratory to the representatives of the churches—all confessions were present at this protest meeting—and to former Secretary of State William M. Evarts.

Grant was a proven friend of the Jews. They had not forgotten how in 1870 he had appointed one of their coreligionists, Benjamin Franklin Peixotto, to the post of American Minister to Rumania. This appointment, made at the height of anti-Semitic excesses in Rumania, was meant as a warning—and was so taken. A few years afterwards William Evarts, then Secretary of State, had expressed the American point of view in unmistakable terms: "This government has ever felt a deep interest in the welfare of the Hebrew race in foreign countries, and has viewed with abhorrence the wrongs to which they have at various periods been subjected by the followers of other creeds in the East."

But that admonition had been directed toward little Rumania. Would equally strong language be addressed to Russia?

Emma Lazarus had come at the invitation of Evarts, whom she had met at social functions. At this time she

BY COURTESY OF THE AMERICAN JEWISH HISTORICAL SOCIETY

EMMA LAZARUS (ca. 1879)

knew very little about politics, but Evarts may well have told her that even for a retired statesman it was no small thing to make a public appearance at such a meeting. Active statesmen, of course, would never have risked it.

The meeting was, as we know, thoroughly anti-Russian in spirit. The selfsame speeches and the selfsame angry outcries from the audience might have occurred in London. But the fact was that official relations between America and Russia were on an entirely different footing from Anglo-Russian relations. During the entire Civil War and later as well, the Czar had shown either benevolent neutrality or outspoken amity. Alexander II had been an admirer of Lincoln. He conceived his liberation of the serfs as a parallel action to the emancipation of the Negro slaves and later, in the presidency of Johnson, he had sold Alaska to the Americans for the ridiculously small sum of seven million dollars.

Alaska had hitherto provided Russia with a base on the American continent uncomfortably close to the Pacific Coast. Her sale of this territory was thus a highly friendly act. It certified that Russia unconditionally recognized the foundation of American foreign policy, the Monroe Doctrine.

How had the other powers acted toward America in these last decades? They, on the contrary, had been as unfriendly as possible. The French had tried to set up a pro-French empire in Mexico. The British had built ships and sold them to the rebellious Southern states; they had almost formally sided with Lincoln's enemies. Curiously enough, these grievances were forgotten at once after the Civil War. The American people did not even realize that Queen Victoria's government had been made to pay a huge compensation for war damage to America—the sum was settled at the time by the Lausanne Conference. That was the government's business; it concerned Washington. The American people felt warmly toward England and things English, just as they did toward things French. Whereas, contrary to the official foreign policy of the government, they hated Russia and the czarist system.

In the mass meeting at Chittering Hall a world issue was at stake. Grant, a semiofficial personage by virtue of his having six years earlier been President of the United States, held his tongue. The Mayor of New York, William R. Grace, contented himself with introducing the speakers and pounding his gavel for order. Evarts, too, was cautious enough to base his condemnation of the pogroms on *English* reports. He spoke of the Christmas pogrom in Warsaw and indicated with what detestation a good Protestant heard of such horrors: "We gather from the *London Times* that three hundred houses and sixty shops were plundered at Warsaw while a garrison of twenty thousand soldiers was kept within barracks—and that on the morning when in the name of Christ peace and good will were proclaimed over all earth." Alas, it was difficult for a man who had only recently served in the government to hurl invective against the internal policies of a friendly state. Moreover, was everything in order within the United States? With astute objectivity the former Secretary of State continued: "Without forgetting the glass house in which we ourselves live—we who have seen anti-Negro riots in New York and anti-Chinese riots at San Francisco—it must still be said that Russia's duty is to civilize herself."

But at this point something amazing took place. The audience at this mass meeting did not want to hear anything about their own shortcomings and the relative merits of American conditions. Liberty must reign on earth! Democracy in America (and how right they were in this) could only be brought to perfection if liberty and the rights of man prevailed throughout the rest of the world. One world! It was a magnificent spectacle to behold how the leadership of this meeting slipped out of the chairman's hands and was taken over by the people themselves, by a host of impromptu speakers.

As Emma Lazarus scanned the auditorium, she could not immediately make out what was happening. A confusion of languages—a dozen tongues were being spoken all at once. First of all, of course, there were the Jews. The tailors and furriers, organized for the past few years and devoted to the cause of socialism, had come out of their sweatshops. The seamstresses and milliners had cousins and brothers left behind in that terrible country of Russia. Now they shouted in Yiddish. Their outcries were heartfelt, more stirring than the polished English of the clergymen. But even louder were the shouts of the German contingent. These people were the Forty-eighters, strapping men with blond beards who had been victims of the German Revolution—a sampling of those hundreds of thousands who had fled to the New World after 1848. These Germans knew their enemy, knew who had rudely shattered their dream of a republic. Never would the Hohenzollerns and their Prussian army have been able to crush the Revolution if the Russian Czar had not stiffened the spine of the King of Prussia. And now a Hungarian shouted in bad English to the excited masses at the meeting; he recounted the atrocities the Russian soldiery had committed in Hungary in 1848, where they had been called in by the Hapsburg ruler. He told about arson, torture, the gallows. And then the Italians and Spaniards spoke up. They too were citizens of New York and had been dipped deep into the melting pot—what resentment could they bear against Russia? But their memories were long. They could not forget that the Czar had stood behind all reaction in Europe. "Save Poland!" a white-haired man cried wildly. Firty-one years earlier he had escaped from the bloodbath of Warsaw, the massacre of Polish patriots by a Russian army. "Save Poland from the enemy of man!" This old man relived it all again. He was not a Jew and had not even noticed that the main task of the meeting was to publish a resolution protesting the persecution of the Jews. What did that matter? This man was protesting for Poland—and therefore for the cause of humanity. For humanity is indivisible.

When the young poet Emma Lazarus returned home through the February night, she knew that the Jewish question involved the problem of humanity.

23

What next took place was strange and difficult to understand. It would be a mistake to term it a "betrayal." It is just another example of how infinite are human potentialities—and also how difficult politics is. And at this time our poet was still a lower-grade student of the hard subject of politics.

The relapse Emma Lazarus underwent during this period did not bring her back to her former attitude of detachment. That would have been impossible after her visit to Wards Island. It was a partial relapse. Her aristocratic temperament reasserted itself, her love for the "chosen people." As a Jew of Portuguese stock she felt herself part of the Jewish nobility; the Jewish tailors and milliners from Poland, on the other hand, were the Jewish masses.

Emma would have been alarmed had she been fully conscious of her true thoughts. But the idea insinuated itself in the disguise of art and therefore her alert conscience was lulled. While her sense of shock at the fate of the masses was completely authentic, another part of her soul was enchanted by the figure of one individual. He was—as almost always in her life—an old man. This time it was Benjamin Disraeli.

The Earl of Beaconsfield had only recently died. Almost at the same time as the news of his death, a book by the Danish Jew Georg Brandes had reached Emma. It described the glorious rise of this baptized Jew, Disraeli, to the position of foremost statesman of the British nation. He, who was himself an Oriental, had surprised the stolid Anglo-Saxons with the command that they must rule the Orient: Asia Minor, Egypt, India and China. He, who had scoffed at the British nobility as an "uneducated caste of hunters, skirt-chasers and gamblers," took pains to dress in their fashion and did not rest until he was accepted as an equal by them—although he delighted in novel-writing, an eccentricity these aristocrats could not comprehend. Having risen from a class of pariahs, the most persecuted of the persecuted, Benjamin Disraeli never tried to lead the pariahs to power (for that would have seemed impossible to him); instead he set himself up as the Tory leader. He made the English Queen, his Queen Victoria who gazed at him out of prominent, pale blue, frequently blank eyes, Empress of India overnight.

This slight old man exercised a magical fascination upon Emma, not so much as a statesman but as an individual. What did she care about his program? She did not know that a statesman can never be described without consideration for the merits of his policies. She wanted to write a novel about him, and was fortunately kept from doing so only by the fretful restlessness that racked her whole being during these months, the mood produced by the unhappy events in the world of Judaism. Instead, she wrote only an essay for the *Century Magazine* entitled, "Was the Earl of Beaconsfield a Representative Jew?" Her answer to this, of course, was yes. But her best friends, among them Rabbi Gottheil, wished she had not written the article. Although it was of course undeniable that the Earl of Beaconsfield represented a section of the Jewish world, it was wrong to insist upon this fact *now*. For now the Jews needed a Moses, a leader of the persecuted masses, not a great courtier who could run the affairs of the Mizraim.

Georg Brandes, who was a good deal cleverer than Emma, had seen Disraeli's unattractive aspects as well as his genius —his crude jokes at the expense of the masses and of democracy, for example. In one of Disraeli's earliest published novels, *The Young Duke*, he had described a writer who on philosophical grounds advocated the removal of mountains. Things that rose too high were useless, he argued; mountains naturally felt themselves to be the aristocracy of the globe—"Down with the Andes and with the Alps!" this rabble-rousing writer cried. Such had been Disraeli's mocking attitude toward the democratic spirit and democratic politics. The people were outside the scope of his understanding. Not irony, but the purest and most rigid earnestness had dictated a youthful poem of his:

>   A band
> Of nobles dignified, and gentry pure,
> And holy priests and reverend magistrates;
> In multitudes thus formed and highly trained
> Of laws and arts, and truthful prejudice
> And holy faith, the soul-inspired race,
> I recognize a People.

Although Emma's better self knew that the people did not at all conform to this picture, the old man's influence overcame her good judgment. Under this influence she could write in her essay:

"He belonged, by birth, to the branch of modern Jews

known as the Sephardim, concerning whom an English writer has remarked: 'Of the two large bodies of European Jews, the Ashkenazim, from Germany and Poland, and the Sephardim, of Spanish and Portuguese descent, it is well known that during the Middle Ages the latter were the more eminent in wealth, literature and importance. The general histories of modern Jews have treated of them as one people per se, without adequate consideration of how differently must have been modified the Judaism of Granada in the twelfth century, or of Castile in the fourteenth century, from that of the same period amid the ferocity and unlettered ignorance of Muscovy and Poland.' There can be no doubt that a spark of fiery Castilian pride was transmitted, unstifled by intervening ages of oppression, to the spirit of Benjamin Disraeli. He knew himself to be the descendant, not of pariahs and pawnbrokers, but of princes, prophets, statesmen, poets, and philosophers. . . ." But what about the folk in Chittering Hall, who were neither princes nor poets?

Later she caught herself up. She criticized Disraeli for his tendency toward self-aggrandizement, "which might also be called vanity," and she even decided that "the study of his career is calculated to dazzle, to entertain, even to amuse, rather than to elevate, to stimulate or to ennoble." But these phrases were extreme and did not represent her real opinion. It was therefore the more dreadful that she was able to continue: "But do all these derogatory facts preclude him from being considered a representative Jew? On the contrary, we think they tend to confirm his title. . . . Where shall we look for the great modern Jews? At the head of the revolutions, the politics, the finance, the journalism of Europe, or among actors, musical *virtuosi* and composers, wherever they can find a field for their practical ability, their long-starved appetite for power, their love of liberty, and their manifold talents. They are on the surface in every city of Europe and America where they have gathered in any considerable numbers. But in proportion as we look among the less brilliant avenues to renown, among the slowly rewarded workers and students, we shall find fewer and fewer representatives of the race."

To print this at that time! And, moreover, in one of the most widely read American magazines. Certainly at that time the issue had nothing to do with virtuosi and composers. A whole people was in exodus, carrying nothing but the attributes of their nationhood. To write of this mass of average men of good will who wanted to live, and as creatures of God deserved to live, that they did not properly belong to the great body of "slowly rewarded workers" who form the rock bottom of the human race—was this not unforgivable folly?

Rarely was folly so quickly punished. The printer's ink was not yet dry when reality gave Emma a smart slap in the face.

24

"Here's something you'll be surprised at." With these words Richard Watson Gilder, editor of the *Century*, handed Emma the issue of the magazine in which her article on Lord Beaconsfield was appearing. The scene was probably the printing plant. Emma had no time to ask what the surprise was. She took her copy and went home.

Richard Watson Gilder and his wife, the brilliant Helena de Kay, were among Emma's best friends. They had set up that Gallic rarity in New York, a salon where lively discussion took place. The salon had come into being quite naturally, for Gilder was not only extremely influential as the editor of a great magazine, the only one which could match

The Atlantic Monthly, but was also the best of hosts. As Theodore Maynard recently described him: "He looked, with his large eyebrows and drooping mustache, a sort of melancholy Robert Louis Stevenson, thin, ascetic, distinguished." In the Gilders' studio all the literary, dramatic, musical and artistic people of the era foregathered; in the eighties and nineties Kipling and Eleanora Duse were to be met there, Madame Modjeska, the tragedian, the young sculptor, Saint-Gaudens, the architect, Stanford White, the graybeard Walt Whitman and the genius of the piano, Paderewski. Often very wealthy people came and contributed money to Helena de Kay's various philanthropic organizations. They were rewarded by the fantastic entertainment of a household where the hosts never slept. At any rate, Richard Watson and Helena relieved one another so that they could keep their "salon" running perpetually, day and night.

At home, when Emma cut the pages of her copy, she was dumbfounded. "By a fateful juxtaposition," as Josephine later called it, Emma found in this same issue an article by a Russian writer, a very noted woman, that defended the Russian pogroms. Oh no, of course, it did not actually defend them, but it explained them—and in this case explanation was virtually the same as vindication.

It was incomprehensible. How could Gilder and his assistant editor, Johnson, be so blind as to let anything like this be printed? "Russian Jews and Gentiles," by Madame Zinaida Alexeievna Ragozin, argued that the pogroms must be looked at "from a historical perspective." There must be a reason, she went on, that all over the world (not only in Holy Russia!) and again and again the people turned against the Jews. The people, Madame Ragozin wrote, aroused by certain Jewish traits, could not help turning against the Jews—for the Jews waged an interminable war against the host people among whom they lived. This war was, to be sure, "hidden," and the very obscurity of it made it all the more sinister. It began thus: the Jews, the "worshippers of the golden calf," everywhere seized upon the gold of the country in which they lived. Small wonder that the poor Gentiles refused to be robbed by the Jews any longer. Why, incidentally, did not the Jews "manfully" defend themselves as soon as they were attacked. (This was a point particularly irksome to Madame Zinaida, since she was the author of juveniles concerning "Aryan heroes" such as Roland and Frithjof the Norwegian.) Her answer to this question was very simple: the Jews cared only about "saving their money"; that was more important to them than manliness and honor.

There were, she continued, Jews who understood the shamefulness of this; a certain Jacob Brafmann, for example, had revealed the truth—that the Talmud itself directed Jews to cheat non-Jews. If, Madame Ragozin concluded, the Jews wanted to go on living in Russia, they would have to stop being Jews; they must abandon their religion and their Scriptures and adopt the "customs of Russianism."

Good God, that was nothing very new. Brafmann, this bought traitor, had lived in all ages. Four hundred years ago in Germany, for example, a converted Jew named Pfefferkorn had denounced the Talmud in similar terms and demanded that every Hebrew book be burned. If the great Reuchlin had not opposed him. . . . But Pfefferkorn and Reuchlin were dead; this Madame Ragozin was still living. Was it possible that some sectors of the Russian intelligentsia agreed with her?

It was not only possible, it was certain. This woman who wrote in English was the western advance guard of a powerful Russian class. Zinaida Alexeievna was a scholar of parts. She was a collaborator on Putnam's huge enterprise of many volumes, *The Story of the Nations*, a member of the Oriental Society, of the Societé Ethnologique de Paris and of the Victorian Institute of London—certainly no feeble antagonist. In her historical works she had already indicated that she could not tolerate the Jews and that she considered them dangerous. In her *Story of Media and Babylon* she had said, in speaking of the decline of the Babylonian Empire: "There was, however, still another influence at work which for being secret, and, so to speak, *underground*, should not be overlooked or underrated: it was the influence of the exiled Jews. . . . They were a power and a danger to the state. . . ."

Just as the Jews were supposed to have invited the Persians into the country to destroy the Babylonian Empire 2,500 years ago, so they were now conspiring with foreign countries to destroy Russia. Zinaida believed this, just as Boris Suvorin, the influential editor of *Novoe Vremya*, believed it, and as did later many among the Nazis. What was the relation between cause and effect, why did the Jews of the Babylonian Captivity feel so antagonistic toward their "host people"—this question these scholars and thinkers did not investigate. Clearly, the fault lay with the Jews!

Emma looked up from the page she was reading. How clearly she could see through it all. The pogroms were not simply "spontaneous outburst of popular rage"; they were part of the intellectual program of Pan-Slavism, part of the program for the regimentation of Russian life and the exclusion of minorities "dangerous to the state." At one and the same time they were an intellectual and a political measure. This justified them in the eyes of a good many Russians —and made them all the more dreadful to American eyes, for America was proud of its minorities and continued to draw fresh strength from the continuous immigration.

All very well. How then, how could the Gilders . . . At

this point Emma at last noticed an editorial comment that she had overlooked. The editors wrote that this contribution had been printed chiefly because of its "extraordinary character," that the charges contained in it sounded "thoroughly medieval," and that the next issue of the *Century* would contain a reply to it.

Emma slipped into her coat. She forgot her hat and her veil. She had only a few blocks to walk, to run. At 13 East Eighth Street the windows of the studio were brightly illuminated. It was around eleven o'clock at night. She thrust her way through the crowd of sandwich-eaters and sherry-drinkers, scarcely greeted her friend, Rose Hawthorne, who gave her a searching glance and said, "You're looking pale, dear Emma." She found Gilder on the point of removing his tie and coat. He was about to take a nap and leave the battlefield of literature to his wife.

"Richard," she said breathlessly, "who is going to answer Madame Ragozin?"

"You, of course," Gilder said.

25

In the May issue Emma's reply was printed. It read like the thunder of big guns.

She had prepared her cannon carefully for a whole month. Historical knowledge, irony, a strict sense of justice, eloquence in the right place—it was all there. When the crash and smoke of the explosion faded, there was nothing left of Madame Ragozin.

No one had ever told Emma that a polemical article had to be brief—if only to give the impression that the author could have said a great deal more. Yet she hit on this principle the first time she attempted the form. "Russian Christianity versus Modern Judaism" proved to be a minor masterpiece even to the way the material was arranged in the allotted space.

So, the learned Russian lady "has for ever demolished, in her mind, the fallacy that the Christians have been persecuting the Jews? She has established in its stead the conspicuous fact that the Jews have been always, and still are, persecuting the Christians, especially in Russia? Can a handful of wretched Jews undermine the well-being of the largest Empire of the globe?"

Whose well-being was really being undermined? Emma answered this question with facts: murder, rape, arson, one hundred thousand Jewish families reduced to homeless beggary, and the destruction of eighty million dollars worth of property—horrors which up to now had been perpetrated only in the darkest days of the Middle Ages.

But was there not *after all* a class of Jews who brought these atrocities upon themselves? Emma now attacked Madame Ragozin's argument about the "two kinds of Jews," the "vast dualism which characterizes the Jewish race." Certainly there were Jews concerned with money and Jews concerned with the things of the spirit, and these Jews were mutually antagonistic—the one group seeking God and the other dancing round the golden calf. But: "The dualism of the Jews," Emma wrote with quiet insight, "is the dualism of humanity; they are made up of the good and the bad. May not Christendom be divided into those Christians who denounce such outrages as we are considering, and those who commit or apologize for them? Immortal genius and moral purity, as exemplified by Moses and Spinoza, constitute a minority among the Jews, as they do among the Gentiles, but here ends the truth of the matter."

And what is the truth about the Talmud, that book so terrible to non-Jews because unknown to them? Madame

Ragozin's charges, Emma wrote, "are singly and collectively false . . . simply a revamping of the wearisome old perversions, garblings, distortions, mistranslations of the spirit and letter of the text. . . ." A trenchant argument occurred to her. "If a Moslem were to print an expurgated copy of the Bible, citing all the barbarous passages and omitting all the humane and noble features, what would Islam think of the cornerstone of Christianity? Yet this is precisely what the Jew-haters have done with the Talmud. Modern philosophical criticism, no less than a study of Jewish history, and a dawning appreciation of the nobility of the Jewish type of character, have dispelled among all thinking and cultivated minds the web of calumny spun by bigotry and folly around these remarkable volumes. . . ."

Possibly Rabbi Gottheil advised her in the writing of this passage; a year later she would herself know Hebrew books in their own language. But whoever lent her assistance with this polemic, the inner dignity of Emma's writing, the composure (and the sadness also) were characteristic of herself alone. They are essentially poetic traits—as, in fact, all true perception can in a sense be said to be poetic. Naturally, her education was also helpful, a thoroughly unusual education. Who else in America had read Belinski, the Russian critic and cultural analyst? According to Belinski, embarrassingly avid haggling took place not only among Jews, but among Orthodox Christian men and women at Russian markets. "When I go shopping in the city, while my ears are deafened and my human dignity is insulted by the vulgar policy of our national business community, advertising its own wares and almost forcibly dragging purchasers into the shops, then do I realize that I have fallen among the greatest swindlers in the world! What is to be done? The Russian is born so! We condemn this Asiatic ostentation, this cringing politeness bordering on servility, this shameless boasting, and can only say, like the fish to the angling-line, it has always been thus in Russia."

Did Emma know that this comment of Belinski's was, of course, as false as all such collective indictments of a people? Probably she did know—she would not have been a poet if she had failed to realize this. But that did not help; Madame Ragozin had fired the first shot against the Jews in this *bataille des dames* and, since Emma had the second shot, she must fire it for the Jews. But did this mean against the Russian? In conclusion Emma used the same words that former Secretary of State Evarts had spoken in Chittering Hall: "It is not the oppression of Jews by Russians: it is the oppression of men and women by men and women. And *we are men and women.*" It was the part of wisdom to have written thus; it was an American conclusion addressed to Americans whose Constitution had sworn to grant equal rights to every living creature.

Madame Ragozin was finished. But the matter itself was not finished. Almost without laying down her pen, Emma wrote two more articles: "The Jewish Problem" and "An Epistle to the Hebrews."

26

A picture stood on Emma's desk. It was the photograph of a gray-haired woman with bright, clear eyes. "That is Marian!" she would say to the friends who visited her in the house on Eighteenth Street where she now lived with her relatives. Her visitors nowadays were still literary people and poets. But in their friendly discussions they no longer dealt only with aesthetic matters. Among them there were social thinkers and philosophers and also publishers like Philip Cowen who wanted to do practical things. Emma, too, was interested in practical activities now. She had only recently written to Philip Cowen suggesting that if his house, the American Hebrew Publishers, intended to publish *Songs of a Semite*, it should do so in the cheapest possible form. "It is my idea to have the pamphlet issued at as low a price and in as simple a form as possible." What did the daughter of Moses Lazarus mean by a low price? "Twenty-five cents," Emma stipulated, and her decision stood. A paper-covered edition, without frills, was to receive widespread circulation.

But who was Marian? Marian Evans had been dead for the past two years. She knew nothing about the exile of the Jews from Russia. But great spirits sense events before they take place. Marian Evans was none other than the great English novelist George Eliot, one who wrote more profoundly and truthfully than most of the literary women of the Victorian era. *Adam Bede, The Mill on the Floss, Romola*—Emma had devoured these novels of hers. But that was not the reason she had Marian Evans' picture on her desk.

Her reason was that George Eliot loved the Jews. George Eliot loved the Jews as such, simply because they were Jews. There was absolutely no reason for this except the two thousand years of persecution the Jews had undergone.

No one loves moneylenders, we think. Emma, who was at this time writing her controversial essay, "The Jewish Problem," for the *Century*, described the historical roots of moneylending. "After being robbed of his lands, he [the Jew] was excluded from all trades and all manual occupation. One alone remained open to him—and this one was *forced upon him by law*—usury." As the learned Rabbi Jacob Tam of France had complained in 1146: " 'We have been left no other branch of industry to support life and to pay the onerous taxes imposed upon us by our landed seigneurs.' "

Emma Lazarus certainly did not *love* Jewish pawnbrokers. But George Eliot, that angel of Franciscan love, even loved *them*. Emma repeatedly read aloud to her friends the passage in George Eliot's *Daniel Deronda* in which the old Jewish moneylender encourages his Christian customer: "Well, sir, I've accommodated gentlemen of distinction— I'm proud to say it. I wouldn't exchange my business with any in the world. There's no more honorable, no more charitable, no more necessary for all classes, from the good lady who wants a little of the ready for the baker, to a gentleman like yourself, sir, who may want it for amusement. I like my business, I like my street, and I like my shop. I wouldn't have it a door further down. And I wouldn't be without a pawn-shop, sir, to be the Lord Mayor. It puts you in connection with the world at large. I say it's like the Government revenue—it embraces the brass as well as the gold of the country. And a man who doesn't get money, sir, can't accommodate. Now what can I do for *you*, sir?"

During the long winter nights when Emma wrote deep into the morning hours (often she began late at night, after her friends had left), she did not set down a word which was not first tested and approved before Marian's picture. Emma tried to judge her own writing as George Eliot would have judged it. She, the Christian, had espoused the Jewish cause; a Jew could do no better than to follow her admiringly.

When Emma, after a night without sleep, wrote down the fateful words: "The Jewish problem is as old as history, and assumes in each age a new form. The life or death of millions of human beings hangs upon its solution; its agitation revives the fiercest passions for good and for evil that inflame the human breast"—an essay of George Eliot's lay beside her, the *Impressions of Theophrastus Such*. There was political journalism that had aspired to and reached the highest levels of ethics. George Eliot was the first to express distinctly and serenely a thought that Jews themselves had not yet ventured to frame clearly: the Zionist program. What was the only way to help the Jews? By resettling them. And this would at the same time help the world, help the nations who were troubled because the Jews would not be assimilated. George Eliot boldly quoted John Stuart Mill who had written in another context: "From the freedom of individual men to persist in idiosyncrasies the world may be enriched." Well then, she exclaimed cheerfully, make use of the Jews' idiosyncratic refusal to surrender their own egos and let them again have the statehood they enjoyed two thousand years ago. "They will enrich the world."

Had not a rebirth of national independence overnight made proud nations of people who for centuries had vegetated in servitude and poverty? "What were the Italians?" Marian Evans exclaimed. "No people, no voice in European counsels, no massive power in European affairs: a race thought of in English and French society as chiefly adapted to the operatic stage, or to serve as models for painters; disposed to smile gratefully at the reception of half-pence, and by the more historical to be rather polite than truthful, in all probability a combination of Macchiavelli, the political cheater, Rubini, the tenor, and Masaniello, the revolutionary of the stage. Thanks chiefly to the divine gift of a memory which inspires the moments with a past, a present and a future, and gives us the sense of corporate existence that raises men above the otherwise more respectable and innocent brute, all that, or most of it, is changed."

The divine gift of memory! Wasn't its power to change being felt currently by every Jew? The actual present held out only miserable prospects for the Jew as soon as it ceased to draw upon visions of the past and the future. Palestine was the past, Palestine was the future; and the present was nothing but a poor way station between these two.

The thought was almost too much for Emma. Tense from so much thinking, writing and debating, from so many nightlong vigils, her heart began to pound so hard that she had to put down the book. But there was no help for it; she must go on. George Eliot had said: "Tortured, flogged, spit upon, the *corpus vile* on which rage or wantonness vented themselves with impunity, their name flung at them as an opprobrium by superstition, hatred and contempt, they have remained proud of their origin." And therefore, it seemed to Emma, they were mature, ripe for the forging of a new nation.

27

"The idea that I am possessed with," Daniel Deronda says at the close of an eight-hundred-page novel, "is that of restoring a political existence to my people, making them a nation again, giving them a national centre, such as the English have, though they, too, are scattered over the face of the globe. That is a task which presents itself to me as a duty. . . . I am resolved to devote my life to it. At the least, I may awaken a movement in other minds such as has been awakened in my own."

Deronda is a rich young man, ignorant of his Jewish origin, who grows up in aristocratic English society, until a succession of inward and outward adventures leads him back to the sources of his being.

George Eliot put into Deronda's mouth her vision of the future of Israel. In February 1883 Emma wrote in the *Century*: "I am fully persuaded that all suggested solutions other than this are but temporary palliatives. . . . The idea formulated by George Eliot has already sunk into the minds of many Jewish enthusiasts, and it germinates with miraculous rapidity." But at once she drew back in alarm. She began to wonder—was what was later to be called "Zionism" the sole solution to the Jewish problem? Emma was an American, and if only for this reason alone she could not believe that. It was not for that that Sephardic Jews had come from Portugal three centuries ago and had become American citizens; not for that were German Jews like Rabbi Gottheil striving for acceptance into American life—not so that all they had dreamed of and accomplished were to be merely incidentals of their journey to the Holy Land. And did the Russian Jews who had been arriving every month for two years—did these thousands want to go to Palestine?

Certainly George Eliot could not see this aspect of it clearly. She had been a native of a nation which itself knew nothing of the sorrows of migration. Therefore she had not understood America, whose historic mission was to be a land of immigrants. America had not ceased and would never cease to be that—or if it did, it would cease to be America. All over the world people were proud of how long they had been established, but in America another kind of pride existed, the curious pride of the "newcomer." George Eliot knew nothing of this, but Emma knew. In her day no one had as yet advanced the hypothesis that Columbus was a Jew who, like other marranos, had fled to sea to escape the Inquisition, thus becoming a discoverer by compulsion. Nevertheless, in her poem "1492" she saw that as a "two-faced year," a year of discovery *and* of persecution.

> Thou two-faced year, Mother of Change and Fate,
> Didst weep when Spain cast forth with flaming sword,
> The children of the prophets of the Lord,
> Prince, priest, and people, spurned by zealot hate.

Hounded from sea to sea, from state to state,
The West refused them, and the East abhorred.
No anchorage the known world could afford,
Close-locked was every port, barred every gate.
Then smiling, thou unveil'dst, O two-faced year,
A virgin world where doors of sunset part,
Saying, "Ho, all who weary, enter here!
There falls each ancient barrier that the art
Of race or creed or rank devised, to rear
Grim bulwarked hatred between heart and heart!"

In this sonnet Emma Lazarus, the Jewish poet, penetrated to the heart of America's mission. Only once more, in the sonnet on the Statue of Liberty, was she so successful in perfectly formulating the meaning of that mission. The dream of Palestine would some day be realized. But Emma understood that Palestine could not be the exclusive reality for the Jews.

The banker Haym Salomon had once given Washington a loan without security or interest to help America's victory, to help her to become the "land of liberty." The Jews who had fallen fighting under Washington and Lincoln had died for this ideal. But the ideal included freedom for them "to remain themselves" and still be Americans. Would anyone wish to give up this right which had been sealed with blood? In 1883 Zionism was purely a problem for the Eastern Jews; the Western Jews had only to continue their struggle for equal *social* rights in the societies in which they lived. And in this respect the Eastern Jews who came to America became Western Jews the moment they entered the country; they stepped directly into the situation created by "American minorities," a social situation which Americans would not allow to become a *legal* problem.

The Jew has long been accustomed to thinking on two

planes simultaneously. He is a dialectician by nature, and destiny repeatedly confronts him with dialectical tasks. Emma Lazarus saw the dilemma correctly; no strict choice between East and West was possible.

In two divided streams the exiles part:
One rolling homeward to its ancient source,
One rushing sunward, with fresh will, new heart . . .

Fresh will, new heart. For the tens of thousands of Russian Jews who had landed on these shores in the past year, a tremendous problem immediately presented itself. Where were they to go to? Amusingly enough, they themselves were not aware of the seriousness of this problem. For to them America was New York. But the American Jews who filled Emma Lazarus' studio with cigarette smoke and animated debate knew how mistaken this was. The Hebrew Immigrant Aid Society and the even more important Montefiore Agricultural Aid Society strove to turn the great tide away from New York, from the city to the farm. "The motives behind the scheme," Raisin writes, "varied from the selfish fear of seeing too many of these Jews inundate the big American cities and thus give rise to a 'Jewish problem' in a land where it had hitherto been nonexistent, to the laudable altruistic desire of ameliorating the dire condition of these refugees."

But it was not easy to induce the newcomers to take up farming. Nor was it easy for them to succeed at it. There was, for example, a man named Rosenthal who had come with the first immigrants. This excellent person, a printer by trade, knew something about agriculture; what was more important, he was a man with a good sense of humor, a joker who was always able to cheer up his fellows. Herman Rosenthal led the first 173 men and women to Louisiana, where they were to settle five thousand acres of farmland. But the houses were so ramshackle they could not be lived in. Julius Weiss of New Orleans furnished the settlers with lumber for building new houses and stables for the horses and cattle. He also supplied new farm implements. But after months of their hard work the Mississippi took a hand, flooded the land for miles around and carried away all they had.

This was one of the typical trials of American settlers. Undaunted, Rosenthal returned to New York the following month and told his sympathetic friends: "Now we will go to South Dakota. There's no Mississippi there." By the summer of that same year Rosenthal and thirty Jewish families were settled in a new colony. They planted oats, wheat, rye and, mainly, flax. But instead of the Mississippi they had the "wheat bug" and, in the third year, drought. For two hundred days the sun burned fiercely and not a drop of rain fell. . . .

In other parts of the Union Jewish colonies flourished. Michael Heilprin, Emma's friend and the author of a book entitled *Historical Poetry of the Ancient Hebrews*, one day showed her a letter he had received from a settler in Texas. "We live a true brotherly life," the settler had written. "Every evening after supper we take a seat under the mighty oak and sing our songs." The letter had a strong effect on Emma. She needed only to close her poet's eyes and she was in Texas.

> Twilight is here, soft breezes bow the grass,
>   Day's sounds of various toil break slowly off,
> The yoke-freed oxen low, the patient ass
>   Dips his dry nostril in the cool, deep trough.
> Up from the prairie the tanned herdsmen pass
>   With frothy pails, guiding with voices rough
> Their udder-lightened kine. Fresh smells of earth,
> The rich, black furrows of the glebe send forth.

> After the Southern day of heavy toil,
> > How good to lie, with limbs relaxed, brows bare
> > To evening's fan, and watch the smoke-wreaths coil
> > Up from one's pipe-stem through the rayless air.
> > So deem these unused tillers of the soil,
> > Who stretched beneath the shadowing oak-tree, stare
> > Peacefully on the star-unfolding skies,
> > And name their life unbroken paradise.

Two thousand years of wandering had formed these people before they found their way to this idyll. No other nation could point to so long a pilgrimage. And they had sought nothing but:

> Freedom to dig the common earth, to drink
> The universal air—for this they sought
> Refuge o'er wave and continent, to link
> Egypt with Texas in their mystic chain,
> And truth's perpetual lamp forbid to wane.

But the majority of the Jews remained in the city, taking on every job they could find. It was not that they disliked the labors of the countryman, but simply that overseas also they had been city folk. Moreover, life was unimaginable to them apart from their relatives and friends, and therefore they clung together in the manner that is possible only to city dwellers. Thus the arrival of the Russians created in the cities of the eastern coast Jewish communities which grew day by day. These people were filled with an eager thirst for justice. Even before the new arrivals could speak a few words in broken English, the quarters of the tailors, cloakmakers, seamstresses and milliners resounded with the slogans of socialism.

What the natives beheld on the streets was an orthodoxy strange to them, whether that of the Talmud or of Marx; the gestures and the language were alien; the ambition of these people was alien; their beelike industry was alien, their refusal to keep normal hours, to take anything "easy." Some, too, brought prejudices with them—and, as Michael Heilprin said, "Prejudice breeds prejudice . . ."

Until 1882 the Jews in America were such a tiny minority that they were overlooked. Now their numbers increased so tremendously that they inevitably altered the quality of American cities. Their neighbors stopped thinking of them as "funny"; anti-Semitism made its appearance. "Since the establishment of the American Union, Jews have enjoyed absolute civil and political freedom and equality, and until the past few years, a large and in some places almost entire immunity from social prejudice," Emma wrote. But that had been true only during the period before the problem of competition became serious. From month to month, however, this problem intensified. A good many Christians (having learned nothing from what they had read in the newspapers so recently) actually began to ask themselves whether these Jews were not criminals or undesirables after all, since they were not wanted in Russia. With concern and unhappy foresight Emma wrote in "The Jewish Problem": "And yet here, too, the everlasting prejudice is cropping out in various shapes. Within recent years, Jews have been 'boycotted' at not a few places of public resort; in our schools and colleges, even in our scientific universities, Jewish scholars are frequently subjected to annoyance on account of their race. The word 'Jew' is in constant use, even among so-called refined Christians, as a term of opprobrium, and is employed as a verb, to denote the meanest tricks. In other words, all the magnanimity, patience, charity, and humanity, which the Jews have manifested in return for centuries of persecution, have been thus inadequate to eradicate the profound antipathy engendered by fanaticism and ready to break out in one or another shape at any moment of popular excitement."

28

In her articles Emma Lazarus revealed a pronounced journalistic flair which would have gone wholly unsuspected in the shy female poet of earlier years. She learned to write with speed, vigor and assurance. When Henry Wadsworth Longfellow died at the end of March 1882, almost the very next day she had prepared a paper on him to be delivered before the Young Men's Hebrew Association. In this paper she had not only to deal with her subject of the dead poet, but she had also to take into account the special character and interest of her audience. With perfect tact and taste she accomplished her task. She first speaks of the poet in general terms:

"He belongs, intellectually and artistically to the generation of Washington Irving, rather than to that of his actual contemporaries, Emerson or Walt Whitman; all his links are with the past; the legendary, the historic, enchanted him with an irresistible glamor; not only was he without the eyes of the seer, to penetrate the well of the future, but equally without the active energy or the passionate enthusiasm of an inspired champion in the arena of the present. A pensive gentleness, a fluent grace, a tender sympathy with the weak, the suffering, the oppressed, with loving women and with little children, and above all, an exquisite delicacy of taste, and an admirable skill of workmanship—these are the distinguishing characteristics of his poetry. He was too sincere to content himself with imported schemes, although he was not sufficiently endowed with original strength to found a new school. Hence, even when he chose an American subject, as in 'Evangeline,' 'Miles Standish,' or even 'Hiawatha,' his point of view and his method of treatment remained essentially European. . . . Here is no painful crudity of rough strength, no intellectual or moral audacity engendered by democratic institutions, and by unprecedented vistas of a broadly developing nationality. All is harmony, sweetness, and purity. Reversing Burns's process of setting new songs to old music, Longfellow, as it were, takes a new tune and adapts it to well-remembered words. One could almost guess from any volume of his poems, what great poet he was reading at the time, and by what foreign influence he was dominated."

At this point we may smile. Did not Emma Lazarus—keen-eyed observer of her own shortcomings that she was—realize that the same stricture could be applied to much of what she had written in the past? She had sometimes immersed herself so deeply in foreign forms and influences that she had lost her own identity entirely. Her Heine parodies (which were not at all parodies) would have made her a member of that famous parody-writing "Echo Club" presided over by Bayard Taylor in the fifties. . . . But since she separated the journalist in herself completely from the poet, it gave her no difficulty to speak of what she considered Longfellow's lack of "original strength."

But at this point Emma was obliged to settle a small score with Longfellow that concerned the Jews. (Since she herself had once written a poem entitled "In the Jewish Synagogue at Newport," there is a personal element here that heightens the interest of the matter for us today who look back on it.) "It is scarcely necessary to recall to Jewish hearers the well-known lines, 'In the Jewish Cemetery at Newport,' wherein Longfellow's tender humanity finds sweet and pathetic expression. These lines, in their almost colloquial simplicity, and their use of sacred, legendary or symbolic terms for purposes of homely illustration, are very characteristic of his method. . . . Jewish readers will not be so willing to accept the concluding stanzas of the poem:

> "And thus forever with reverted look
>   The mystic volume of the world they read,
> Spelling it backward, like a Hebrew book,
>   Till life became a legend of the Dead.
>
> "But ah! what once has been shall be no more!
>   The groaning earth in travail and in pain
> Brings forth its races, but does not restore,
>   And the dead nations never rise again."

These are pretty verses, but they are simply not true—so thought Emma Lazarus. And so she immediately added: "The rapidly increasing influence of the Jews in Europe, the present universal agitation of the Jewish question, hotly discussed in almost every pamphlet, periodical and newspaper of the day, the frightful wave of persecution directed against the race, sweeping over the whole civilized world and reaching its height in Russia, the furious zeal with which they are defended and attacked, the suffering, privation and martyrdom which our brethren still consent to undergo in the name of Judaism, prove them to be very warmly and thoroughly alive, and not at all in need of miraculous resuscitation to establish their nationality."

Like every writer with a real streak of the journalist in him, Emma Lazarus loved the atmosphere of the printing office. She was impatient to see her thoughts transformed and materialized into the dully gleaming lead type. Printers don't like authors hanging about one bit—Philip Cowen must have liked Emma very much indeed when he later described one of her unexpected visits: "I shall never forget one such visit. I had taken down a printing press to clean. I looked like a dozen printer's devils rolled into one. Old clothes, hands and face black with smudge, I felt rather uncomfortable. But Miss Lazarus refused to hear my apology, saying that if she broke in on me at such an inopportune time, she was the one who should apologize." But a far more important incident occurred when Cowen, apparently bringing proof sheets, visited her at her home: "I well remember," he relates, "the sting in the remark of a sister as she came into their home one day with one of the sons of Charles A. Dana of the *New York Sun*. As they went upstairs, possibly in reply to a curious look towards me, the sister said: 'Yes; that's Emma's Jewish editor.' " It is astonishing that such a scene should have taken place in the home of Moses Lazarus. Even if we allow for the possibility that Cowen, a man risen from the position of an artisan, might have felt uncomfortable in the surroundings of such wealthy bourgeois, a man such as he was must be trusted. The incident really did occur, and it was doubtless Annie Lazarus who planted the sting in the visitor's soul. She was the one who later broke away from Judaism. Long after her father's death, of course. Terrible things would have happened had she looked askance at Jewish things or persons in his presence. It is curious that Moses Lazarus at that time seemed almost a more fiery advocate of the Jewish cause than Emma herself. He would be thrown into a rage by trifling matters certainly not worthy of great notice. When, at a dinner party, Henry Ward Beecher repeated to his illustrious English guest, Herbert Spencer, the old quip as to why God should choose the Jews, Moses Lazarus was up in arms and at once sent a bristling communication to the *American Hebrew*.

29

The father! *Still* the father? Seven years after Emerson has ceased being Emma's spiritual guide, Moses Lazarus' position is once again unshakable. This father fixation of hers will now last until the old man's death. But now the relationship has lost a good deal of its psychological danger. The wall separating Emma from the rest of the world has been breached; the ivory tower she had inhabited both as artist and person tumbled down before the blast of her awakened Jewish consciousness.

The outer world? It is curious that a person like Emma, whose activities obliged her to speak to hundreds of people, had no real place of her own. She continued to live in her father's house, and whoever came to see her had to see her there.

The real reason for this was never suspected by the people close to her. If one had said to Emma that it would have been more suitable for a writer of her caliber to live alone, she would probably have answered that it was not a "ladylike" thing to do. *Une vie à la garçonne?* Why? Ever since the great Aurore Dudevant, who wrote under the name of George Sand, had passed through Europe with a troupe of friends and lovers—Musset and Chopin *inter alios*—important female writers were thought to be people without any ties who traveled a lot, drank and smoked, and whose hearts "were to let at least twice a year."

This conception of the female author was of course as false as the notions of decorum opposed to it. It is by no means certain that a family life in the midst of wealthy bourgeois and the moral ideas of the plush era were more befitting to an independent spirit. There are bold ideas that cannot be thought when one sits down three times a day at table with the face of one's respectable middle-class father and a pack of sisters opposite one. It has been often remarked that Emma did not translate Heine's "freest" poems. She was a masterful translator of his verse, even a

What was the American interest in this? According to Oliphant, "Russian Jewish emigration to America is attended with many disadvantages, and the American Government is therefore anxious to cooperate with the Russian to find a better field of emigration and one which would at the same time subserve the interests of Russia in the East."

Imagine: Emma Lazarus subserving the Russian interests in the East! Such was the squalid nature of politics at that time already, a bargaining with human souls. You had to have strong nerves to stand it.

No, Emma Lazarus' nerves were not strong enough. She was a warrior of the Lord—but when she read in the papers that her idol Sarah Bernhardt, the great French actress, had been bodily attacked as a Jewess by a Russian mob in Odessa and had barely succeeded in escaping to her hotel, then Emma wept for shame. For she was and remained a woman, above all. And so, somehow, it was good that she lived in her father's house as in a castle, shielded from that dangerous outer world—a castle, but a prison too. She probably felt both these aspects of her situation acutely. For in those years (at least until her first trip to Europe), we know, Emma was very unhappy. The violence with which she flung herself into her political and cultural activities often looked suspiciously like flight. But whom was she fleeing from? From herself? From which of her selves?

What must she have felt, for example, when her eyes encountered the picture of George Eliot on her desk—the picture of a woman who, next to her father, was probably the person she loved the best. This woman had plunged not only spiritually but personally into the midst of the world and had flinched from nothing. She had not only hatched emancipated thoughts, but had also lived an emancipated life—not for the sake of the body, but of the spirit.

When in 1842, Marian Evans, then twenty-two years old,

decided to go to church no more—she was then under the influence of Charles Bray, an English positivist (and was shortly to translate works by the German religious rationalists David Friedrich Strauss and Ludwig Feuerbach)—she had first to break with a beloved father, a pious man of the Church of England. The break was healed; her father's failing health, above all, brought her back under the parental roof. During the seven years that she nursed him, however, her opinions did not alter a jot. Shortly after his death she went to the Continent, to Geneva, city of refuge. When she returned to London she had to stand on her own feet, she of whom Bray said that "she was not fitted to stand alone. . . . She was always requiring some one to lean upon." She obtained the post of assistant editor of John Chapman's *Westminster Review*. She even lived in the same house that held the editorial offices, 142 Strand—for she believed that she belonged nowhere else and that where her mind dwelled, there must her body dwell too. A woman entirely given over to literature? Just here, however, in the editorial offices, through Herbert Spencer she one day met George Henry Lewes, biographer of Goethe, critic, sociologist and natural scientist. She not only fell in love with this married man, but lived with him, for more than two decades, until 1878, when her dearly beloved Lewes died.

This step of course closed the door of every "respectable" house in Victorian England to Marian Evans; yet she never regretted it. Even those who pardoned her her "sin," could not pardon her the perfect happiness she enjoyed. Lewes was criticized far more than she. In the eyes of his contemporaries, as Margaret Lonsdale says, he "must have possessed a more than common share of the selfishness of men in general, or he could not have deliberately cast a moral and social blight upon George Eliot's life, by inducing her to stifle her womanly nature so far as to consent to live with him in dishonour." This "dishonour" she steadfastly ignored. It was *this* man whom she loved and whom she needed near her in order to write the great novels of George Eliot. What she needed was not the "emancipation of the flesh" preached in France, but this perfect union with the man who could sustain and encourage her in her work. And this could only be brought about by living together with him. A narrow circle of unprejudiced and accomplished people was able to appreciate this.

The celebrated Marian Evans was no masculine spirit, but an utterly sensitive and tender woman, prone to frequent fits of depression and, like Emma, to "agonies of shyness." And yet she had entered on this marriage which was no marriage in the legal sense; she had sacrificed her "security as a woman" for the sake of a spiritual ideal. Without Lewes, without her hearing him stirring about in the next room, we should not have her novels today.

Even the first step in this remarkable life—the break with her father—would have crushed Emma Lazarus. She was never able to immolate herself for the sake of what she considered to be her task, as George Eliot had done. And perhaps she was right. Perhaps fate acted kindly toward Emma in sparing her the necessity of choosing. How kind, we can see by glancing at the life of a remarkable American woman who in many respects was Emma Lazarus' predecessor, in other respects almost her double, and then again a malicious parody of her. We are speaking of Adah Isaacs Menken.

This Southern girl, thought by some to have been the daughter of a Spanish Jew named Ricardo Fuertes, grew up in New Orleans. At the age of twelve, she not only showed proficiency in modern languages, but also began a translation of the *Iliad*. She knew Hebrew and the Bible. The good education she had acquired was the subject of remark by her friends, and by her enemies as well. A Parisian journalist, after an interview with her, wrote: "She knew and talked on every subject with giddying facility, from the dialects of the New World to transcendental mathematics, from Latin to philosophy, from versification to theology." These words have an unpleasant ring. Such words would have hardly occurred to a journalist in the case of Emma Lazarus, whose deep and universal cultivation astonished everybody who frequented Richard and Helena Gilder's salon.

Adah Menken's first husband was the musician Alexander Menken (her second was a prizefighter). With him, in 1858, she went to Cincinnati where she came under the influence of Rabbi Isaac Mayer Wise, editor of *The Israelite* (how strangely similar to Emma's career!), and wrote her first Jewish poems, dedicated to the past of her people. The prophecies of the return of Israel to the holy soil had instilled her with a faith in the messianic redemption of the Jewish people. In one of her poems she exclaims:

> Will he never come? Will the Jew
> In exile eternally pine?
> By the idolaters scorned, pitied by a few,
> Will he never his vows to Jehovah renew
> Beneath his own olive and vine?

In another poem she sees herself in Jerusalem, dwelling in a tent—

> On the dust where Job of old has lain,
> And dreamed beneath its canvass walls
> The dream of Jacob o'er again.

But the anticipations of the poetry that Emma Lazarus later was to write go much further. When Adah Menken first heard of the Mortara case—on June 23, 1858, the child Edgar Mortara of Bologna had been violently removed from the custody of his Jewish parents and forcibly baptized—

140

she staunchly issued a call to the people of Israel all over the world:

> Brothers awake, strike high and strong
> For danger that may come.
> Strike high for Israel's holy right
> And strong for hearts and home.
>
> Lift the white flag that was unfurled
> O'er Israel of yore.
> Let the cry of God and our right
> Echo from shore to shore.

Is not this really an embryonic version of Emma's famous "The Banner of the Jew," with its electric first lines: "Wake, Israel, wake! Recall to-day / The glorious Maccabean rage"? Emma Lazarus never read Adah's lines, and she hardly knew of her existence. But the remarkable similarity between the two women extended further. Adah Menken, too, engaged in journalistic polemics. When for the first time a Jew was admitted to the English Parliament, *The Churchman* wrote that "there is a bitter curse hanging over England, and Queen Victoria is doomed to eternal perdition in consequence of the admission of Baron Rothschild into the House of Parliament." She answered this with a forceful article.

But now we come to the decisive difference between Emma's predecessor and herself. There coexisted in the woman we have already described another woman with the soul of a star of the variety stage. When still half a child she had danced on the stage in New Orleans together with a sister named, like Emma's sister, Josephine. She worked her way up through a series of bad plays and bad theaters to the position of an international celebrity who was acclaimed everywhere. The *Court Journal* of London had this to say of her: "Menken is the fashion of the Metropolis. She is the most talked of actress in London, and in society, at the clubs, in the streets, the name of Menken reigns supreme." Another paper added, "The public watch her day after day. . . . Duchesses, even if they are young and beautiful, pass unnoticed when La Belle Menken is in sight."

In the days of her Byronomania Emma had preferred above everything his *Mazeppa*. Now La Menken wound up her career with the performance of a ballet-like play derived from the *Mazeppa*. When Adah came on stage bound half-naked to the back of a horse, a huge scandal was the result which Bernard Falk has described in his book *The Naked Lady*. "My costume," she wrote, in reply to criticism, in a newspaper, "or rather want of costume as might be inferred, is not in the least indelicate. . . . I have long been a student of sculpture, and my attitudes are selected from the works of Canova. . . ." At another time she even wrote to a magazine: "I am a thinking, earnest woman, and in that line alone I wish to be spoken of."

In 1868, after a hectic career, at the age of only thirty-three, she died in Paris. Through all the wild ups and downs of her life she never forgot that other self which slumbered within her and to which she dedicated the moving verses of "My Heritage":

"My heritage!" It is to live within
The marts of Pleasure and of Gain, yet be
No willing worshiper at either shrine;
To think, and speak, and act, not for my pleasure,
But others'. The veriest slave of time
And circumstances. Fortune's toy!
To hear of fraud, injustice, and oppression,
And feel who is the unshielded victim.

What would Adah Menken have said if she had been offered Emma Lazarus' sheltered existence, with a father as the sole center of her life? She would certainly have said no—just as Emma would have said no to the life of Adah Isaacs Menken.

30

The day has twenty-four hours. But if we work as if it had thirty-six—what will happen to the abused body? In these past two years Emma had overstrained herself. She looked paler and frailer than ever; her blue-gray eyes had a moist, unearthly brilliance.

It was not writing that was wearing her out. It would have been impossible for her *not* to write. From November 1882 to February 1883 she published her *An Epistle to the Hebrews* in sixteen sections. She borrowed the title from Paul's Epistle in the New Testament. Where previously she had directed her writing chiefly to non-Jewish critics or to friends of Judaism, she now wrote right to the hearts of the Jews; she taught her people to perceive their own dignity and warned them of the great peril they would encounter if their enemies should prove able to vindicate even a single point of their many charges.

Her own body was weak, but she implored others to strengthen theirs. "Antipathy to manual labor is one of the great social diseases of our age and country. . . . What we need . . . is the building up of our national, physical force. If the new Ezra arose to lead our people to a secure house of refuge, whence would he recruit the farmers, masons, carpenters, artisans, competent to perform the arduous practical pioneer-work of founding a new nation? . . . For nearly nineteen hundred years we have been living on an Idea; our spirit has been abundantly fed, but our body has been starved, and has become emaciated past recognition, bearing no likeness to its former self."

Was wealth the way to win respect? In America particularly, "in the midst of this feverish, speculating, half-educated . . . Plutocracy," the path of wealth was the worst of all and was sure to incur hatred. Liberty and equality were novel possessions to the Jews. "What wonder," Emma wrote in her *Epistle*, "if an overweening arrogance and ostentation were among the first outward tokens of emancipation from oppression and contempt? What wonder if in a people confined for centuries by foreign legislation to the lowest by-ways of petty traffic, we should find wits sharpened to super-subtlety by long practice in the arts of chaffering, bargaining and acquiring? What wonder if in the hearts of a people who for over a thousand years had found no other bulwark than wealth against the murderous hatred of Christendom, the desire of accumulating wealth had grown to be an hereditary instinct and one of the strongest passions.

"And yet such were far from being the *normal* instincts and passions of the Jews. The Talmud says: 'Get your living by skinning carcasses in the street if you cannot otherwise; and do not say, I am a priest, I am a great man, this work would not befit my dignity.'"

For her quotations from the Talmud Emma had at first to rely upon Rabbi Gottheil. But for a year now she had been studying Hebrew with Louis Schnabel, a Parisian. Acquiring languages had never been difficult for her—she already commanded five or six. It was far harder for her to translate thinking and writing into practical action. When it became necessary to urge the State Department to do something for the Jews, Emma Lazarus was expected to do it. And it was likewise taken for granted that she would personally collect money for the newly established Jewish Technical Institute. And yet she was shy and could not appear in public. When a Philadelphia society requested her to deliver a lecture on the Jewish situation, she answered: "I beg to say in reply that anything in the nature of a lecture or an address is entirely beyond my province and capacity." She would gladly write an address, but someone else would have to deliver it.

This fine woman, who was scarcely ever alone, whom people thronged to, lived, inwardly, in the deepest solitude. Her friend, Rose Hawthorne, the daughter of Nathaniel Hawthorne and herself a writer, later recounted: "Miss Lazarus and I sometimes walked and talked together (after meeting in the Gilders' salon). And she had such sweet delicacy of spirit that she never gave the least sign that she did not find a very secure footing for her mental exploration while accompanying a person who knew little Latin and less Greek. On the contrary, she assured me that I was a paragon for 'stirring her up with suggestions.' I doubt if two more fundamentally disconsolate minds could have been found in the whole world than hers and mine."

Disconsolate? We should imagine that Emma would have found great satisfaction in her work on behalf of the Jews. But her dissatisfaction with herself—five years earlier John Burroughs, Whitman's friend, had warned her against it—was still boundless. Her dissatisfaction sprang from an urge to perfection—always, whatever she did seemed to her imperfect. Now, strangely enough, at the time of her most intensive activity in the cause of Judaism, this urge prompted her to redouble her interest in other cultures.

Since first seeing the Italian actor, Tommaso Salvini, on the stage ten years before, Emma had held him in high esteem. When he came to New York a second time, between October 1882 and April 1883, her friendship with him reached its culmination. The great tragedian had won her heart with his performance of—we again have cause to smile—King Lear, as the father of a Cordelia, that is. And Emma, of course, once more fell into the role of daughter. Since Salvini could not speak a word of English, he needed to be guided through the mazes of Manhattan by Emma. (On the boards of the Fifth Avenue Theater he had declaimed alone in Italian amid an all-English cast.) The actor was grateful and displayed regal surprise when, for a banquet at the Hotel Brunswick, she translated his "feeble speech" into the best of English. John Sullivan read the speech; Emma—if present at all—did not dare to open her mouth, of course.

At this time Tommaso Salvini was probably one of the greatest actors of the world. His letters in Italian are chiefly about himself, scarcely ever about her—although once, writing from St. Petersburg, he praised her *giusto criterio, intelligente analisi, e la poetica forma.* Her contact with him presumably encouraged Emma to dream about the presentation of a dramatic work that she had begun some time ago, but had completed only one year before. It was *The Dance to Death,* a play about medieval Germany.

31

The first time we hear of *The Dance to Death* is in a letter dated May 25, 1882, that Emma Lazarus wrote to Philip Cowen: "A few years ago I wrote a play founded on an incident of medieval persecution of the Jews in Germany, which I think it would be highly desirable to publish now, in order to arouse sympathy and to emphasize the cruelty of the injustice done to our unhappy people. I write to ask if the American Hebrew Publishing Company will undertake to print it in pamphlet form. I send you also a poem which I should be glad to have you publish, if you can make room for it. Will you kindly return it if you do not care for it? It has a strong bearing on the question of the day, besides having a curious historic interest."

We may be permitted to cast some doubt on one phrase in this letter—"a few years ago." Though Emma's statements about her own writings are generally completely reliable, it is probable that, feeling a bit ashamed, she wished to conceal how late in life she had become concerned over the fate of the people of Israel. There is some evidence that her play could not have been conceived or written *before* the Russian pogroms. Among others, there is this minor, but important indication: the fiercest persecutor of the Jews in her play bears the name of Dietrich von Tettenborn. Now Tettenborn is not a name to be found in Germany proper. It is a name found only among the Baltic German nobility, and almost all the governors and generals of modern czarist Russia who persecuted the Jews were Baltic barons!

The scene of the play is Thuringia, in the May days of 1349. Emma knew this small German province from Wagner's opera *Tannhäuser*, as well as from her own romantic story about the adventures of that minnesinger. But the fate of so many Jewish literary artists—that sooner or later the beauty of the world is rent and it is revealed in all its true horror—weighed on Emma's play as well. She may have sighed: "Is there really no spot on earth where a Jew has *not* suffered?" So even the lovely Thuringian forests in her play are no longer the forests of the troubadours; their branches supply the wood for the flames of autos-da-fé.

In a succession of powerful scenes the tragedy of the Jewish community of Nordhausen is laid bare. The Jews are accused by their enemies of having brought the plague, the Black Death, into the countryside by poisoning wells and rivers. "I have seen," one of the characters of the play recounts,

> yea touched the leathern wallet found
> On the body of one from whom the truth was wrenched
> By salutary torture. He confessed,
> Though but a famulus of the master-wizard,
> The horrible old Moses of Mayence,
> He had flung such pouches in the Rhine, the Elbe,
> The Oder, Danube—in a hundred brooks,
> Until the wholesome air reeked pestilence;
> 'T was an ell long, filled with a dry, fine dust
> Of rusty black and red, deftly compounded
> Of powdered flesh of basilisks, spiders, frogs,
> And lizards, baked with sacramental dough
> In Christian blood.

At the beginning of the play, the Jews of Nordhausen foolishly believe that they will be spared, because as money-lenders they are indispensable to the prosperity of Nordhausen community. Then in masterly fashion the dawning perception of their true situation is described. Two Jews converse together on their way to the synagogue:

BARUCH: What said you of this pilgrim, Naphtali?

. . . .

NAPHTALI: He comes from Chinon, France,
Rabbi Cresselin he calls himself—alone
Save for his daughter who has led him hither.
A beautiful, pale girl with round black eyes.
BARUCH: Bring they fresh tidings of the pestilence?
NAPHTALI: I know not—but I learn from other source
It has burst forth at Erfurt.
BARUCH: God have mercy!
Have many of our tribe been stricken?

NAPHTALI: No.
         They cleanse their homes and keep their bodies
               sweet,
         Nor cease from prayer—and so does Jacob's God
         Protect His chosen, still. Yet even His favor
         Our enemies would twist into a curse.
         Beholding the destroying angel smite
         The foul idolator and leave unscathed
         The gates of Israel—the old cry they raise—
         We have begotten the Black Death—*we* poison
         The well-springs of the towns.
BARUCH: God pity us!
         But truly are we blessed in Nordhausen.
         Such terrors seem remote as Egypt's plagues.
         I warrant you our Landgrave dare not harry
         Such creditors as we.

Then, inside the synagogue, Rabbi Cresselin of France, acting like the messenger in a Greek tragedy, warns the Jews of Nordhausen of their impending fate. They must flee! He recounts what he himself witnessed in Cologne. The frightful scene springs frightfully to life:

The venerable Mar-Isaac in Cologne,
Sat in his house at prayer, nor lifted lid
From off the sacred text, while all around
The fanatics ran riot; him they seized,
Haled through the streets, with prod of stick and spike
Fretted his wrinkled flesh, plucked his white beard,
Dragged him with gibes into their Church, and held
A Crucifix before him. "Know thy Lord!"
He spat thereon; he was pulled limb from limb.
I saw—God, that I might forget!—a man
Leap in the Loire, with his fair, stalwart son,
A-bloom with youth, and midst the stream unsheathe

> A poniard, sheathing it in his boy's heart,
> While he pronounced the blessing for the dead.
> "Amen!" the lad responded as he sank,
> And the white water darkened as with wine.

With his last strength Rabbi Cresselin utters these words:

> God's angel visited my sleep and spake.
> "Thy Jewish kin in the Thuringian town
> Of Nordhausen, shall be swept off from earth,
> Their elders and their babes—consumed with fire.
> Go, summon Israel to flight—take this
> As sign that I, who call thee, am the Lord,
> Thine eyes shalt be struck blind till thou has spoken."

And hardly has he spoken when he falls dead! A horrible panic fills the synagogue. Should they believe the dead man's words? Or is not his death rather punishment for his having been the carrier of mad rumors? The majority of the Jews decide, though with heavy heart, in favor of the latter.

Now an intrigue begins, as ill-conceived as in most nineteenth-century historical dramas. Prince William of Thuringia, the son of the old Landgrave, is in love with Liebhaid, the daughter of Süsskind von Orb, the wealthiest and most powerful man in the Jewish community of Nordhausen. Needless to say, Prince William's plot to rescue the fair Liebhaid and her Jewish tribe miscarries; the whole love story is as unconvincing and dull as Emma's love plots generally are. More important, however, is the fact that at this juncture a man embodying Emma's conceptions of Jewish dignity rises to the heights of grandeur. In the person of Süsskind von Orb, a patriarch in his sixties, we again behold an idealized version of her father. When the Jews are already doomed to die, when all is virtually lost and a last plea is made before the fiendish council of burghers, old

Süsskind delivers a speech that is as masterly in its logical force as in its human truthfulness, a speech that is among the best things Emma Lazarus ever wrote:

> Noble lords,
> Burghers and artisans of Nordhausen,
> Wise, honorable, just, God-fearing men,
> Shall ye condemn or ever ye have heard?
> Sure, one at least owns here the close, kind name
> Of Brother—unto him I turn. At least
> Some sit among you who have wedded wives,
> Bear the dear title and the precious charge
> Of husband—unto these I speak. Some here,
> Are crowned, it may be, with the sacred name
> Of Father—unto these I pray. All, all
> Are sons—all have been children, all have known
> The love of parents—unto these I cry:
> Have mercy on us, we are innocent,
> Who are brothers, husbands, fathers, sons as ye!
> Look you, we have dwelt among you many years,
> Led thrifty, peaceable, well-ordered lives.
> Who can attest, who prove we ever wrought
> Or ever did devise the smallest harm,
> Far less this fiendish crime against the State?
> Rather let those arise who owe the Jews
> Some debt of unpaid kindness, profuse alms,
> The Hebrew leech's serviceable skill,
> Who know our patience under injury,
> And ye would see, if all stood bravely forth,
> A motley host, led by the Landgrave's self,
> Recruited from all ranks, and in the rear,
> The humblest, veriest wretch in Nordhausen.
> We know the Black Death is a scourge of God.
> Is not our flesh as capable of pain,

> Our blood as quick envenomed as your own?
> Has the Destroying Angel passed the posts
> Of Jewish doors—to visit Christian homes?
> We all are slaves of one tremendous Hour.
> We drink the waters which our enemies say
> We spoil with poison,—we must breathe, as ye,
> The universal air,—we droop, faint, sicken,
> From the same causes to the selfsame end.
> Ye are not strangers to me, though ye wear
> Grim masks to-day—lords, knights and citizens,
> Few do I see whose hand has pressed not mine,
> In cordial greeting. Dietrich von Tettenborn,
> If at my death, my wealth be confiscate
> Unto the State, bethink you, lest she prove
> A harsher creditor than I have been.
> Stout Meister Rolapp, may you never again
> Languish so nigh to death that Simon's art
> Be needed to restore your lusty limbs.
> Good Hugo Schultz—ah! be those blessed tears
> Remembered unto you in Paradise!
> Look there, my lords, one of your council weeps,
> If you be men, why, then an angel sits
> On yonder bench. You have good cause to weep,
> You who are Christian, and disgraced in that
> Whereof you made your boast. I have no tears.
> A fiery wrath has scorched their source, a voice
> Shrills through my brain—"Not upon us, on them
> Fall everlasting woe, if this thing be!"

But all in vain. Nothing can move those stony hearts. To all that has been said Tettenborn has only this to say:

>   No more, no more!
>   Go, bid your tribe make ready for their death
>   At sunset.

And now Süsskind finds words which for nobility are comparable to that famous scene in Schiller's *Maria Stuart* where the unhappy Queen of Scots deplores the "indecent haste" with which her adversaries prepare her death.

>At set of sun to-day?
>Why, if you traveled to the nighest town,
>Summoned to stand before a mortal Prince,
>You would need longer grace to put in order
>Household effects, to bid farewell to friends,
>And make yourself right worthy. But our way
>Is long, our journey difficult, our Judge
>Of awful majesty. Must we set forth,
>Haste-flushed and unprepared?

Again in vain. The raging mob is already howling in the streets, piling up fagots for the bonfire. However, the last scene but one, in the synagogue, shows that the Jews of Nordhausen are worthy of their leader Süsskind. Their hearts are lifted up to God. They resolve to meet death not only with pride, but attired as if for a joyous festival:

>. . . let us crave one boon
>At our assassins' hands; beseech them build
>Within God's acre where our fathers sleep,
>A dancing-floor to hide the fagots stacked.
>Then let the minstrels strike the harp and lute,
>And we will dance and sing above the pile,
>Fearless of death, until the flames engulf,
>Even as David danced before the Lord,
>As Miriam danced and sang beside the sea.
>Great is our Lord! His name is glorious
>In Judah, and extolled in Israel!
>In Salem is his tent, his dwelling place
>In Zion: let us chant the praise of God!

And in this fashion they die. They die with pride, they die as dancers in their festal clothes, with cymbals and lutes in their hands, men and women as well as children. And what was holiest to them they take with them in their death. It is a magnificent vision:

>Bring from the Ark, the bell-fringed, silken-bound
>Scrolls of the Law. Gather the silver vessels,
>Dismantle the rich curtains of the doors.
>Bring the perpetual lamp; all these shall burn,
>For Israel's light is darkened, Israel's Law
>Profaned by strangers.

Once, in 1869, Emerson had warned Emma: ". . . the sole advice I have to offer is a pounding on the old string, namely, that though you can throw yourself so heartily into the old world of Memory, the high success must ever be to penetrate unto & show the celestial element in the despised Present, and detect the deity that still challenges you under all the gross & vulgar masks." Emma should have kept this warning in mind when she wrote *The Spagnoletto*. At that time she still had nothing to say. But now, when she wrote *The Dance to Death*, she had a great deal to say. The "despised Present" grins horribly at us; "the gross and ugly masks we behold" are the fearful countenances of the czar, of Hitler and his crew. . . . Here Emma had successfully written a work that was thoroughly contemporaneous, a work into which she poured the eloquence and wisdom of her Jewish forefathers, their knowledge of doctrine, nobility and death. It was a work upon which the shadows of Gabirol, Rashi, Halevy and Spinoza rested; and it also showed that rare Jewish joy in beauty which is so often overlooked or considered Greek.

Emma may well have dreamed of Salvini in the part of Süsskind of Orb—but the play never reached the stage because it was not really a stage play. None of the dramas of the Victorian era was written or even conceived for the theater. The very eloquence so prevalent in those plays prevented their presentation. Some of the better Victorian poets really seemed to think they held in their hands the key to "writing like Shakespeare"—but did they? Shakespeare, it is true, can be eloquent to the point of grandiloquence; but never unless the character really requires it. Emma and her contemporaries, however, spoke correctly and loftily under *all* circumstances; they did not know how to introduce pauses, did not understand that only a pregnant silence stamps a speech as truthful. These are, to be sure, mere formal details—but in art form is decisive.

When the play, written at long intervals, was at last finished, Emma dedicated it "in profound veneration and respect, to the memory of George Eliot," to her beloved Marian who had upheld the Jewish cause. A terribly busy winter followed. And then the event so long overdue occurred. It was not a nervous breakdown, not a matter of taking to bed and having doctors. It was simply that Emma's consciousness of self vanished. Suddenly she could no longer understand what it was that had so occupied her for years. She had to lay down her pen and flee, go to sea, go anywhere, to some place where Emma Lazarus, the champion of the Jewish cause, was not.

It was, certainly, not self-deception when she informed herself and others that she had to go to England immediately to win over influential Britons to the support of the Jewish cause.

But the bios within her knew better. Again in her life the hour had struck.

BOOK THREE: LITTLE TIME WAS LEFT

Come closer, kind, white, long-familiar friend,
    Embrace me, fold me to thy broad, soft breast.
Life has grown strange and cold, but thou dost bend
    Mild eyes of blessing wooing to my rest.
So often hast thou come, and from my side
So many hast thou lured, I only bide
Thy beck, to follow glad thy steps divine.
    Thy world is peopled for me; this world's bare.
    Through all these years my couch thou didst prepare.
Thou art supreme Love—kiss me—I am thine.

32

On a fine day in May 1883 a woman of thirty-four sailed from New York. Her family, who stood waving their handkerchiefs on the pier, did not suspect that she had little more than four years to live. She herself did not know, but fate knew. And because it happened, we too know. And we know also that therein lay tragedy; she would never fulfil herself.

To outward appearance she was an ordinary vacationer. She wore the costume of the eighties, which prescribed anonymity. Only at home and in the salon was a woman then a distinct personality. On a voyage and especially on the deck of a ship she was only a human figure in a Scotch cap, a warm plaid coat and a veil that the sea wind played with and blew slantwise and behind her. The wind came from the bow of the ship, from Europe, and the fluttering veil held the promise of the future.

The waves rose, the waves fell; when the sun shone through a gap in the clouds, the waves appeared blue-black in the distance; on fair days the sea was bright blue and like a mirror. But most of the time there was a stiff breeze and the ship moved through water that was like greenish-black malachite with white fractures showing.

Emma carried with her a cargo of vague thoughts about

herself, about her accomplishments and her reputation as an English poet.

Emma had written in the English language about her people, the Jews. The Jews were her own people, no doubt about that. But did that make them her readers? Here was a disturbing problem: the Jews who had poured into New York in such numbers had not only a different level of culture, but also, surprisingly enough, belonged by temperament to an altogether different class from that of the romantic and elegiac poet. Humor is indispensable to literature in the *galut*. Out of laughter at themselves and their enemies the Jews gathered courage. But Emma, although in conversation she sometimes came out with a well-turned Heinean quip, was in general incapable of such laughter. Her verses have an intransigent, Old Testament seriousness.

The Jews are a conservative folk. In a mood of devotion, they open the Bible, the Talmud and the great writers of the Middle Ages. What could a contemporary contribute in the way of seriousness? Humor was what was wanted from a Jewish writer of the eighties, whether it was ghetto humor or that characteristic "grinning grasp of triviality." Emma had never had any feeling for the comic aspects of everyday life, for the charming self-deprecation of the individual Russian Jew. When she saw the "little stories" with which even so serious a man as her Hebrew teacher, Schnabel, amused himself and others she felt rather sorry for his "descending so low." For she always thought of the Jews as "a people" and spoke of them in poetical, lofty language. What she forgot was that no Jewish work written about the *galut* started out in the solemn vein—although it might very well come to that in the end; its point of departure was always the little man, the Jewish tailor, petty bourgeois, proletarian, and their joys and sorrows. The fact that Emma did not know how to do this—that she could not write, for example, like Sholom Asch—restricted her reading public. The Jews that read some, but not all of her Jewish poetry, esteemed her merely for her pro-Jewish politics. Since no significant reading public for Emma's poems grew up among the Jews, it was not likely that they would interest non-Jews for long. To non-Jews they remained limited and specialized in their subject matter, interesting just so long as the particular political problem of the Jews was current. (Even a man like Henry George wrote to Emma: "You should not write songs for *your* people, but for *the* people.") It was precisely this that was tragic, for in the Songs of a Semite Emma had for the first time achieved complete poetic command of the English language. In those poems she freed herself of her earlier youthful faults of precocity and dilettantism.

Not that this was the first instance of striking competence. For in the invisible baggage which she was taking with her to England was one professional asset that no one could deny her. She was a translator of the very first rank; few persons in her time could compare with her. Her grasp of the essence of foreign languages was phenomenal. From Musset and Hugo she had learned to feel her way to the core of French. Her translations of Heine from the German, issued in a special volume in 1881, were unsurpassed. (Stedman had jokingly suggested that she append to her name the degree, T.O.H.—"Translator of Heine.") Interestingly enough, what she learned from the Italian made the greatest contribution to her own command of English. In this, her experience was like Dante Gabriel Rossetti's; as soon as the outlines of English words were placed against the luminous field of Italian poetry, the English appeared purer and more fragrant. From Petrarch and Dante Emma learned how to write English poetry.

But these things were past for the moment and now she

stood at the rail of the ship, beside young Annie, her sister, whom she was taking out into the world for the first time. A damp wind moistened Emma's brows and the dark down along her cheeks. The years of overwork had markedly affected her appearance, even her eyes seemed extinguished. But now her natural grace returned. She was filled with excitement; in a little while, the sailors had told her, Ireland would appear out of the mists. ". . . a shadow on the far horizon, like the ghost of a ship," she wrote home; "two or three widely scattered rocks which were the promontories of Ireland, and sooner than we expected we were steaming along low-lying purple hills."

It had originally been planned that Rose Hawthorne should accompany Emma on this first trip of hers to Europe. (At least, Rose had confided on April 11, 1883, in a letter to Thomas Bailey Aldrich that she would spend the whole summer with Emma Lazarus in Europe.) Rose was a very nervous person, fond of speaking of herself as being "disconsolate"; there was something in her of her father's dark moods, and of her grandmother, who, for forty years had not left the room in which her husband had died. She would have scarcely been the right companion for Emma, who was beset by her own anxieties, and it was probably for the best that Rose Hawthorne did not after all accompany her.

The voyage was a pleasant experiment in spiritual realities. England, did it really exist, the England of her youth, the England of her childhood dreams, speaking the pure accents of her years of yearning? Now she would find out.

33

"England is a garden," Emerson had once noted with amazement. "Under an ash-colored sky, the fields have been combed and rolled till they appear to have been finished with a pencil instead of a plough. The solidity of the structures that compose the towns speaks the industry of ages. Nothing is left as it was made. Rivers, hills, valleys, the sea itself, feel the hand of the master."

An American could scarcely help feeling this. To one coming from the Western Hemisphere, from a "vigorous and noisy nation," the first impression was one of being plunged into a potent stillness, into the midst of a painted scene. Everything seemed suddenly silent, speaking only to the sense of sight. Frenchmen were even more amazed and uneasy about this. Hippolyte Taine, descended from a nation of talkers, never felt really at home in England because "English taciturnity" was so alien to him.

It was not quite so alien to Emma. During the shyest periods of her childhood she had incessantly daydreamed about being an Englishwoman. Now she found that the landscapes of which she had dreamed actually existed. Everything was there as she had pictured it; but at the same time it had the silvery remoteness of pictures.

Emma in her youth had taken comparatively little pleasure in visual experience. Like most romantic poets, like introspective people in general, she had been far more addicted to music. Music is the most subjective of the arts, painting the most objective. As Goethe well knew, young people rarely have an understanding of painting. First the "tumult of the ego" must cease, before a man acquires the coolness and composure to see the world as a landscape.

Emma had undoubtedly felt her lack of visual sensitivity, and the urge to perfection had led her to stress color values in her early poems. Thus she described the moments before sunrise:

> Above the shadowy world
> Still more and more unfurled,
> The gathered mists upcurled
>   Like phantoms melt and pass.
> In clear-obscure revealed,
> Brown wood, gray stream, dark field:
> Fresh healthy odors yield
>   Wet furrows, flowers, and grass.

This was observation of the rare, private moment. But on her first day in England Emma noted that Chester, with its quaint streets, was "like the scene of a Walter Scott novel, the cathedral planted in greenness, and the clear, gray river where a boatful of scarlet dragoons goes gliding by." Here was something novel, the awakening in her of a sense of the color of everyday things, an ability to observe ordinary life. When, a few days later, she passed through London like a painter, through, as Josephine later recounted, "the bewilderment of London, and a whirl of people, sights, and impressions," it was this very sense of color that stood as a guard between her and the outer world. She would have been thrown off her feet and swept away had she not, for the first time, exercised this "coolness of vision."

And Josephine adds, "She was received with great distinction by the Jews, and many of the leading men among them warmly advocated her views." Letters from Rabbi Gustav Gottheil, Michael Heilprin and others had preceded her; but her principal recommendation was the *Songs of a Semite*. England was the land where George Eliot had written her *Daniel Deronda*, from which Laurence Oliphant had sailed to the Holy Land to study the possibilities for establishing Russian Jews there. But in those June days of 1883 Emma's chief preoccupation was with matching her childhood dream of England against the reality. And she was not disappointed. Not only did they exist, these people and poets to whom she had once looked up, but she felt herself their equals. When she went with Annie to lunches and teas to which she had been invited by no effort on her part—she was showered with invitations from people like Edmund Gosse and Henrietta Huxley—she found men and women, says Josephine, strongly attracted by her, by the force of her intellect, by her brilliant conversation and at the same time by her simplicity and childlike enthusiasm. But apparently what most impressed London literary society was her sense of dignity. She could not contradict, of course, all the stories current about Emerson's loss of memory, for they were true. But when she was asked at a party whether it was really true that the old man (dead then for a year), in making a speech at Longfellow's funeral, had stared into the coffin and had begun: "I've known him these forty years; and no American, whatever may be his opinions, will deny that . . . that . . . that . . . *I can't remember the gentleman's name* . . . was a truly great man" —then Emma gave her questioner a chilly look and retorted briefly: "And don't you think that the speaker *also* was a great man?"

In England her customary shyness left her. On June 17 she made the acquaintance of Edward and Georgiana Burne-Jones; a week later she met Robert Browning for the first time.

34

Robert Browning received Emma Lazarus with great kindness. Evidently the great poet had not been offended by what the *Westminster Review* had written about Emma fifteen years before: "Admirers of Browning will, we know, think we are uttering something akin with blasphemy, when we say that the *Admetus* of Miss Lazarus will in some points bear comparison with *Balaustion's Adventure*. . . .:" It was nonsense, of course, comparing Browning with an untried beginner like Emma—but Browning had forgotten the matter or, what was most likely, had never even read the item. In other respects, however, he knew a good deal about her. And he did not consider her interest in things Jewish "clannish." It coincided, in fact, with his own interest. One day Thomas Hardy would overhear Browning and Emma Lazarus argue about the meaning of a Hebrew sentence; Browning then conceded that "she knew the tongue better than he." With some pride he showed her Elizabeth Barrett Browning's marginal notes in her Bible; she too could read Hebrew. He could have added that—according to the letters his late wife wrote to her sister Henrietta between 1846 and 1859—"going to Jerusalem" was a cherished dream of their married life.

What Emma did not know was that Robert Browning since his childhood had mixed with Jews and was familiar with their customs and modes of thought. He was the son of a bank clerk in the employ of Rothschild; this fact accounts for his lifelong friendships with Jews of every rank— merchants and scholars such as Martin Philippson, and members of the English aristocracy such as Lady Battersea, Sir Julian Goldsmid and Sir John Simon the physician. When the first reports of the Russian pogroms reached London, Browning had boiled over with rage; he had immediately signed his name to a list of those who advocated English intervention in the matter. Though Browning was kindly disposed to Emma's poetry, there is no doubt that his sympathy for her had been awakened more by the fact of her being a Jewess. He once remarked that he had always felt himself drawn to "artists and Jews," and particularly so when the Jews were the artists. When Sir John Simon says in this connection that it was probably Emma Lazarus who stimulated Browning to compose his talmudic poems, we must approach this statement cautiously. At the time Browning made Emma Lazarus' acquaintance in 1883, he had already been for decades an informed admirer of Jewish culture and hardly needed any encouragement from her side.

Browning the writer of lyric poems was—as Emma knew—a kind of masquerader, and jester too. Once, in one of the love poems to his wife, he had written:

> What are we two?
> I am a Jew,
> And carry thee, farther than friends can pursue,
> To a feast of our tribe;
> Where they need thee to bribe
> The devil that blasts them unless he imbibe
> Thy . . . Scatter the vision forever! And now,
> As of old, I am I, thou art thou!

Already in New York Emma had puzzled over this. Browning a Jew? Was it possible? Certainly *not*. (Here she was not so naive as Browning's friend and first biographer, Mrs. Sutherland Orr, who, perhaps misled by Browning's fondness for spiritual disguise, took his "Jewish ancestry" seriously.) But what, really, could Browning have meant by the line "I am a Jew"? Philip Cowen too was perhaps puzzled, not only by this line, but also by other riddles in Browning's poetry and he asked her to question Browning in order "that the members of the American Browning Clubs might be relieved in their literary distress." When Emma in London then queried the master as to what he had meant, he parried the question with a smile and said: "How can I recollect to-day what I had in mind forty years before when I wrote these lines?"

Emma Lazarus' first meeting with Robert Browning was to have taken place at the home of Mrs. Anne Skepper Procter, a lady whom Henry James described in a letter to Emma as "a wonderful old person and a great friend of his, living in her flat at the top of a high Apartment House." On Sunday afternoons, he added, Browning was sure to be there. But at the last moment the meeting did not come off for some reason (Mrs. Procter, who was already very old, was perhaps indisposed), and the poet wrote to Emma inviting her to visit him in his own home where he and his sister Sarrina would expect her for tea.

When Emma for the first time crossed the threshold of Browning's house, he was no longer "a man in the highest physical spirits, with a torrential vitality bounding and bouncing over the place," as the Hawthorne family in 1858 had seen him in Florence. He was now seventy-one years old—that is, we may be permitted to remark, the perfect age for calling forth in Emma all her love and veneration.

Such might very well have happened, if there had not been another person ruling over the house at 19 Warwick Crescent who forbade it. Browning was a widower. But, though she had been dead these twenty years, the great personality of Elizabeth Barrett Browning breathed still within the house and touched everything with its presence. Nothing was changed in her room and his; her portrait looked down from the wall, with its delicate, suffering, narrow Creole face, watchful, as if she were shielding her husband against the adulation of all the lady members of the countless Browning Clubs in England and America. . . .

Emma knew everything Rose Hawthorne told about the wonderful woman who had been the queen of Browning's heart for so many years. Once Mrs. Browning had taken Rose on her lap, but the girl—looking at her heavy, dark curls and white cheeks and great dreamy eyes—had wondered whether this wraithlike person was really alive. Later on Rose even managed to speak almost disrespectfully of "her enormously thick-lipped mouth and her hand like a bird's claw." Although Emma rated beauty in women very highly, she did not miss it in this case; out of deep reverence she almost dared not touch the things that had belonged to Elizabeth Barrett, things her friendly host showed her: piano scores . . . a lace shawl . . . those French bibelots and that sweet bric-a-brac of Paris which Elizabeth had called the "mire of the Seine" . . . a Chianti glass from which she had drunk . . . vistas of Pisa and Florence that she had collected . . . ("Italy! Italy!" was the sigh Browning vented at every tenth phrase). But when he opened a little phial, that still held the fragrance of those old days, this contact with Elizabeth Barrett seemed almost too corporeal to Emma; she shrank back and turned her head away. There was a lump in her throat, she later said, for awe.

There are some noteworthy parallels between the lives of the two women, parallels that Emma in all likelihood knew nothing of. On the light side, there is the fact that the Barretts of Wimpole Street, like the Lazarus family, owed their fortune to American sugar. There is the more serious fact that Elizabeth, in spite of all her poetic precocity, had been nothing more than a "father's girl" until her thirty-eighth year. Mr. Barrett had been a true autocrat (what Mr. Lazarus had never been) who never could see why his daughter should marry. Her father used her poor health as a pretext to secure his domination over her. Elizabeth's body, "hardly more than a transparent lamp" (as O. H. Burdett put it), was racked continually by illness. When she reached the age of thirty-two, it seemed that tuberculosis would shortly carry her off—but it did not. The unforeseen occurred: a man burst into Elizabeth's life and took her away, from family and from disease. They eloped to Paris, and later went to Italy. He was Robert Browning, a man who was—how seldom is this the case!—exactly like his poetry. The impact of Browning's poetry on Emma had always been great—but more from the human than from the artistic side. When, after Emma's death, John Greenleaf Whittier and others spoke of the particular influence Browning had exerted on Emma Lazarus' lyrics, they were for the most part mistaken. Indebted as she was to Browning's example in the handling of the dramatic soliloquy—it is apparent in her "Death of Raschi"—nevertheless there is nothing of the Browning spirit in her poems. Emma's own verses, both the good and the bad, were born out of a genuine solemnity. But Browning was not solemn. She could admire his riotous rhymes and, in many of his poems, almost Falstaffian high spirits, but only from a distance; it was foreign to her own nature. It was a new thing in lyric poetry to conclude an exposition of the most difficult and controversial notions with a hearty laugh, as Browning did. This had nothing to do with the angry wit of Emma's beloved Heine, which was merely the other side of a "pathos" of growing bodily and spiritual pain. There was no pain in Browning. His lyrics were hale and hearty, enjoying almost middle-class good health. Perhaps she envied him it; but living in that realm of beauty which Shelley and Byron had inhabited, she could not even approach Browning's realistic and generally half-humorous speech.

When Browning said in *Paracelsus:*
> I cannot feed on beauty, for the sake
> Of beauty only; nor can drink in balm
> From lovely objects for their loveliness

—Emma at a certain time in her life could have calmly answered: "I can. . . ." But when he later wrote down his childhood memories in such verses as these of his "Asolando"—

> My Father was a scholar and knew Greek.
> When I was five years old, I asked him once,
> "What do you read about?"
>   "The siege of Troy."
> "What is a siege and what is Troy?"
>   Whereat
> He piled up chairs and tables for a town,
> Set me a-top for Priam, called our cat
> —Helen, enticed away from home (he said)
> By wicked Paris, who couched somewhere close
> Under the footstool, . . .
>
> . . . .
>
> This taught me who was who and what was what:
> So far I rightly understood the case
> At five years old: a huge delight it proved
> And still proves—thanks to that instructor sage,
> My Father, . . .

then Emma, reading them, could only gasp in amazement at the similarity to experiences of her own with her father. But to set them down on paper with such warmth and humor would have been entirely beyond her. And she would never have seen Helen in a cat.

But such matters as these were hardly the subject of conversation of her first visit to Robert Browning. Later visits followed. It is difficult to believe that Emma, after paying repeated calls on Browning, did not detect what was really the most noteworthy thing about him. Browning was what thousands of poets have *not* been: the poet of marital life. He wooed Elizabeth long after she became his wife, his whole life through. And she wrote the greatest love letters of English poetry, disguised as "sonnets from the Portuguese," to him. Emma Lazarus was now almost thirty-four years old, yet no man had broken into her heart there to wrestle with the image of her father. Every meeting with Browning, that great poet of the love of man and wife, must have reminded Emma that she was a spinster. . . . There was only one remedy at the moment, an excellent one: to think that she was a "traveler" only, a visitor who would pass on.

35

On July 14, Bastille Day, Emma made a brief trip to the Continent, to Paris—and she was frightened. She did not know why. This certainly was not the Paris she had dreamed of, not the sweet and melancholy Paris of Alfred de Musset whose "Nuit de Mai" and "Nuit d'Octobre" she had translated so marvelously. Had she perhaps a foreboding that she was some day to be more unhappy in this "City of Light" than in any spot on earth? Or was it the sudden break from that aristocratic English calm she had found so congenial? In her childhood she had been so fond of French that she had even written a little poem in the language:

>C'était au mois de Mai,
>Je te voyais, mon amour,
>Et la Nature souriait,
>Tu me parlais bas ce jour.
>Les ondes, les roses, les fleurs,
>Et les oiseaux dans leur nid,
>Ecoutaient tous, ce jour,
>Le mot que tu m'as dit.

It manages to recapture a little of the tenderness of a French folk song. But now the French seemed to her a people vegetating in a barren country ruined by high politics. She went to Versailles and found it no more than a "gorgeous shell of royalty, where the crowd who celebrate the birth of the republic wander freely through the halls and avenues, and into the most sacred rooms of the king." She recoiled from Paris itself. "There are ruins on every side . . . of the Commune, or the Siege, or the Revolution; it is terrible—it seems as if the city were seared with fire and blood."

So she returned to England which now—how strange!— seemed after a few days absence like home to her, and justly named Old England. How thoughtlessly one sometimes spoke this phrase. What was so strange and yet so familiar about England was the manner in which the inhabitants accepted the most modern, most progressive and comfortable forms of life side by side with a spirit that was very old indeed. The railroad passed through a countryside dotted with ivy-covered houses and sometimes stopped in the middle of a field by an ancient well. One could get out and drink in the silence as Shakespeare and Byron might have done on this very spot. Emma drove through Surrey, and through Kent, "where the fields, valleys and slopes are garlanded with hops and ablaze with scarlet poppies." Flowers, flowers everywhere. The whole country was fragrant with them, and everyone, no matter what his occupation, seemed to have some near or far relationship to gardening. The cathedral at Canterbury loomed suddenly before her, looking just like some old picture—and yet, with its rose window in full blaze, it belonged in the summery present. Emma saw Windsor and green Oxford with its colleges. The evening sun of July fell through the windows of a library and made golden letters glint on the brown backs of books. Stratford upon Avon, Wells, Exeter and Salisbury; Shakespearian names, haughty names, counties and towns for whose possession dukes and pretenders had once drawn their swords. As an American Emma had never before had really ancient land underfoot; the experience now made her reach "a crescendo of enjoyment." She could not see enough of it. She saw York, Edinburgh, the south of Scotland, before she sailed home, leaving behind the happiest four months of her life. But they remained in memory, and therefore she still possessed them.

36

She carried back with her something that had an enduring effect upon her. This was her friendship with the poet and social reformer, William Morris.

She had met him at the home of Burne-Jones, and at first a memory of old embarrassment may well have made Emma shy with him. For William Morris was the poet whom Howells had accused Emma of feebly imitating. The slur had hurt her so deeply that when her *Admetus* and "Tannhäuser" were published in book form, she had appended a note stating that at the time these works were written she had not been familiar with Morris's "Love of Alcestis" and "Hill of Venus." But this old insult was soon forgotten when she met Morris face to face.

She visited him at least twice in his curious workshop which was half factory and half monastery ("a place which hangs doubtful between the past and the present," he himself had modestly characterized it) on July 6 and August 20, 1883. And she at once felt a sense of fraternal relationship with this strange man.

In what way fraternal? William Morris, fifteen years older than Emma, had also been a frail child who grew up in libraries. Locked within the world of words, Morris had been virtually blind to things outside of books. The first attempts at liberation were made by the eyes and by his nervous, eager fingers simultaneously. Morris had seen old tapestries in encyclopedias; he had seen pictures of people in medieval dress, the houses in which they lived and the cathedrals in which they prayed. And the beauty of these things had so overwhelmed him that one day he resolved to be an architect and craftsman, a master with his hands, rather than of the mind.

Naturally, he became a poet nevertheless. Together with the painters Ford Madox Brown, Burne-Jones and Rossetti he established a firm "to combat the immeasurable ugliness of modern life." They made new rugs, chairs, chandeliers, wall coverings; but for a long while their productions were not appreciated. How long could people go on living in such ugliness? While Morris the poet was reveling in Icelandic sagas, living at Arthur's court, and in the world of Virgil, Morris the social reformer was discovering that capitalistic mass production had destroyed the intimate and loving relationship between the worker and the objects he created. Day by day everything in the world was getting uglier.

But the objects themselves were already revolting against this state of affairs. They broke easily, tore, no longer served their function. "We have to go back to the origin of things," Morris passionately explained to Emma. "I have tried for instance to make woolen substances as woolen as possible, cotton as cottony as possible. . . . I have used only the dyes which are natural and simple, because they produce beauty almost without the intervention of art. . . ." Spurred on by these ideas, William Morris had set up the workshops of Merton Abbey, where he himself was foreman and the workers shared in the profits.

To Morris nothing seemed more shameful than the "abuse" of men or materials. But now, as he led Emma through his factory, he confessed to her that profit sharing and the tiny medieval community of craftsmen could not be a final solution for him. At this very time Morris was approaching a fateful decision. He was considering his resignation from the democratic federation which he himself had helped to build, and the founding of a socialist league. This step would take the aesthetician out into the politics of the street, would plunge him into banned meetings. Blows would rain, he would be arrested and dragged away by the police as had been John Ball, the medieval revolutionary. All the while Morris would go on writing pre-Raphaelite books, books dedicated to the worship of beauty —and would permit no one to say that there was a contradiction in these activities.

"Poetry for the few?" he thundered (he spoke to Emma in the same vein as in his lecture before the Trades Guild of Learning). "I do not want art for a few, any more than education for a few or freedom for a few. No, rather than that art should live this poor, thin life among a few exceptional men, despising those beneath them for an ignorance for which they themselves are responsible, for a brutality which they will not struggle with; rather than this, I would that the world should indeed *sweep away all art for a while*."

To this point Emma had listened with unquestioning admiration. But now she ventured a sisterly smile. Really, this man was her brother! She herself, although strongly attracted by some socialistic traits of the Mosaic Law, was not a socialist—but as a Jewish nationalist she knew very well why such highly strung persons as herself or William Morris had to join mass movements sooner or later—in fact, had to *lead* mass movements. Not that, in their hypersensitivity, they would ever be "objective." But they would suffocate in the "prison of words" and in the solitude of their own egos if they did not create palaces, cities of God in which they could live together with others.

Morris was the only person to whom Emma drew close

in England. Closer even than to Browning. With Morris alone her perpetual timidity lapsed and she told him about her childhood. Among other things, she spoke of her childhood Anglomania and of her experience with the teacher who looked like a young angel. But for Morris we should be ignorant of this tale. For later he spoke of the matter to one of his disciples, William B. Parnes, who knew and admired Emma, too—and from Parnes, a very old man, the author of this book heard the story in 1939.

37

Emma had been back in New York only six weeks when an appeal came to her from a committee that was planning to set up, on Bedloe Island in New York harbor, a colossal statue, "Liberty Enlightening the World." Some decades earlier two Frenchmen had conceived the idea of this statue, Laboulaye, the statesman, and Auguste Bartholdi, the sculptor. These two Frenchmen, apparently ashamed of the unfriendly policies the French Empire had pursued toward Lincoln's America, wished to "conciliate" the Americans. They therefore planned this gift which should remind America of the better France of Lafayette's time. The Americans were taken by surprise; they had no need of being "conciliated" because they had never been angry with France.

The statue, which was being built in Paris (it was really more of a construction job than sculptor's work), grew to incredible dimensions. How was it ever going to be transported? The famous Trojan horse was a tiny mouse compared to it. Was not the handling of the statue an immigration problem in itself? But the very vastness of the conception ("the biggest statue in the world") inflamed the ambitions of the Americans. Overnight, everyone was in favor of it. "Liberty Enlightening the World" entered the arena of politics like a kind of golem before it was ever set up. New York, which had originally been lethargic about the whole affair, stiffened its back when it saw that the other "cities of liberty," Philadelphia and Boston, were indicating a desire to obtain the colossus for themselves.

The request to Emma came from the chairman of the committee, her old friend, William M. Evarts. Money was needed to build the pedestal for the statue, and as one of the fund-raising projects an auction was to be held, in a gallery on the corner of Fourth Avenue and Twenty-third Street, at which manuscripts of Longfellow, Walt Whitman, Bret Harte and Mark Twain were to be sold. Evarts asked Emma to contribute a manuscript for this purpose, and after some hesitation she sent the committee a sonnet. Probably she hesitated because she saw in this request to write "to order," for a specific purpose, an infringement upon her cherished "liberty of invention." But was not the idea of Liberty in all its majesty more important than a petty set of artistic liberties? In any case, she sat down and, in the last week of November 1883, wrote fourteen lines that have become immortal.

THE NEW COLOSSUS

Not like the brazen giant of Greek fame,
With conquering limbs astride from land to land;
Here at our sea-washed, sunset gates shall stand
A mighty woman with a torch, whose flame
Is the imprisoned lightning, and her name
Mother of Exiles. From her beacon-hand
Glows world-wide welcome; her mild eyes command
The air-bridged harbor that twin cities frame.

Sonnets.

I.
The New Colossus.

Not like the brazen giant of Greek fame,
  With conquering limbs astride from land to land;
Here at our sea-washed, sunset gates shall stand
A mighty woman with a torch, whose flame
Is the imprisoned lightning, and her name
Mother of Exiles. From her beacon-hand
Glows world-wide welcome; her mild eyes command
The air-bridged harbor that twin cities frame.

"Keep, ancient lands, your storied pomp!" cries she
With silent lips. "Give me your tired, your poor,
Your huddled masses yearning to breathe free,
The wretched refuse of your teeming shore.
Send these, the homeless, tempest-tost to me,
I lift my lamp beside the golden door!"

1883.
  (Written in aid of Bartholdi Pedestal Fund.)

BY COURTESY OF THE AMERICAN JEWISH HISTORICAL SOCIETY

"Keep, ancient lands, your storied pomp!" cries she
With silent lips. "Give me your tired, your poor,
Your huddled masses yearning to breathe free,
The wretched refuse of your teeming shore.
Send these, the homeless, tempest-tost to me.
I lift my lamp beside the golden door!"

This poem has become a part of world literature. One of the most remarkable aspects of the poem was the fact that Emma had never seen the statue when she wrote the sonnet, had never seen the burning torch of liberty shedding its light through the salty air of New York harbor upon the "huddled masses" of immigrants. The statue stood in a shed in Paris and she knew it only from photographs and wooden models.

How did she know that the New Colossus would stand in forcible contrast to the classical Colossus of Rhodes alluded to in the first line? No matter—however it was that she knew, in the shadow of this poem all question of Emma's earlier weaknesses fades away. In this her strength sufficed; this was the *overflow* that William James required when he wrote her: "The power of *playing* with thought and language . . . ought to be the overflowing of a life rich in other ways." For it was the *experience* of the idea embodied in the statue that made the poem possible.

There were some who thought Emma's poem more articulate and architecturally greater than the planned statue itself. Old James Russell Lowell, at this time American ambassador to England and a poet who had formerly not thought too highly of Emma, wrote to her: "I liked your sonnet about the Statue much better than I like the Statue itself. But your sonnet gives its subject a *raison d'être* which it wanted before quite as much as it wanted a pedestal. You have set it on a noble one, saying admirably just the right word to be said, an achievement more arduous than that of the sculptor."

38

But now "fate knocked at the door." The phrase is Beethoven's. And in the three years before her death Emma no longer played Schumann; at the piano she turned only to Beethoven and Bach.

"Fate knocked at the door." After an unproductive winter which proved that the English journey had not relaxed but had overtaxed her, she fell ill. In the summer of 1884 she herself was convinced that she was very sick. We do not know what her symptoms were—but Emma's narrow shoulders and her boyish, undeveloped body must have caused tuberculosis to be suspected. When she finally got well again, she was weary as never before in her life. And hard upon the heels of this illness, while she was still numbed from it, her father died. The family, as the end approached, stood in despair round his bed, Emma more stricken than the others. For—Josephine saw this clearly—"her father's sympathy and pride in her work had been her *chief incentive* and ambition, and had spurred her on when her own confidence and spirit failed." For whom else had she lived? He was the first to whom she proudly showed letters from her great contemporaries—what Henry George had written to her and the eight letters from Henry James. Her father's influence may have seemed to diminish in latter years, but this was an illusion. Moses Lazarus was still the only man in Emma's life. When she saw his face on his deathbed, she spoke two lines of the poem by Poe she most loved:

Ah, broken is the golden bowl! the spirit flown forever!
Let the bell toll!—a saintly soul floats on the Stygian river.

Since her childhood Emma had stood on terms of rhetorical familiarity with death, and this relation had often inspired her to write very good poetry, and sometimes very bad poetry, such as her elegy on the death of President Garfield. But it was something different to meet with a death after which "life lost its meaning and charm." How true the words of John Burroughs must have sounded to Emma now, the sympathetic lines he had written to her long after the death of his own parents: "I am always thankful for any word or remembrance that makes my tears flow afresh. Ones capacity for sorrow exhausts itself after a time, & his feelings become benumbed, & he grows indifferent. But by & by some word, or look, or gesture, or incident of his father or mother comes suddenly back to him, & the thought that they are forever gone becomes incredible, & for a moment his grief is as acute as ever. Even at this date I often start up from my chair in the solitude of my study, & say, it cannot be, it cannot be. . . ." But it *was*. Emma never got over it.

Eight weeks after her father's death she traveled to Europe to "recover herself." She did not succeed. Old England, the home of the Brownings, which was to become almost her own home—nothing there was as it had been, not even William Morris. She tried to overcome her state of inward hollowness by undertaking a novel, though the form was one in which she had worked so seldom. But after the first chapter she laid it aside. "I have neither ability, energy, nor purpose. It is impossible to do anything. . . ."

In the autumn she fled to the Continent. In Holland she at last really awoke. In New York she had fallen in love with some pictures by Delacroix. At The Hague and in Amsterdam she now saw, perhaps for the first time, originals of Rembrandt and other Dutch painters; her sense of sight experienced a bacchantic intoxication and she wondered whether she ought not to become a painter. She bought canvas and paints. After all, her English friends were all practitioners of several arts at once. Why not she? She felt filled with renewed energy.

Emma went on to France, to a Paris that lay at her feet in a golden autumn, with copper trees, its twisting stream, its enchanting galleries and bookshops. On Montmartre she wept for joy. No, she would not join Heinrich Heine in the grave.

Had she recovered? She traveled on to Italy like a bird of passage. The Mediterranean shimmered in the sunlight.

39

In her love for Italy Emma Lazarus was not only influenced by the strong interest taken in Italian culture by such New England writers as Longfellow, Hawthorne, Lowell, and Margaret Fuller (who had prevailed upon Emerson to read Dante), she was even more in this respect a disciple of Browning.

The fact that Emma's reveries more readily took shape as poetry on Italian soil—as in the somewhat conventional poem "A Masque of Venice," wherein Death, masked as a nobleman, takes possession of the heart of a beauty, or in the lengthy epical poem "Saint Romualdo," which describes the wild youth of a man who later grows pious—is not so important as the fact that she was already an accomplished translator of Petrarch when she first set foot in Italy. Max I. Baym, who devoted an essay to these translations entitled A *Neglected Translator of Italian Poetry: Emma Laz-*

arus, intimated that her friend Thomas Wentworth Higginson had in all likelihood urged her to read and to translate Petrarch. Higginson's article, "Sunshine and Petrarch," which had appeared in 1876 in *The Atlantic Monthly*, was undoubtedly known to Emma. But her first "spiritual visitation" by the genius of Italy had probably taken place in her reading of George Eliot's *Romola*, which had been brought out in installments by the *Cornhill Magazine* in 1862–63. Emma was then fourteen years old. But, impressionable as she was, there is hardly any doubt that she was able to grasp, even at that age, the discussion, in *Romola*, that Bardo holds with his daughter concerning the nature of poets and poetry. ". . . it was almost," writes Baym, "as if Bardo addressed at the same time another invisible daughter in remote America: 'For me, Romola, . . . it was with the great dead that I lived; while the living often seemed to me mere spectres—'" But why spectres? Not only because they were "shadows dispossessed of true feeling and intelligence," but because the canon of Greek beauty had begun to vanish from the world of the living. Beauty in the abstract meant a great deal to Emma (as it did to most of the Victorian poets), but one cannot help noticing, too, that the older she got, the more her conception of the Beauiful was exclusively concentrated in the female body. Firenzuola's famous Renaissance essay, *Della Bellezza delle Donne* ("On the Beauty of Women") was well known to her, and her translation of that sonnet by Petrarch on the dead Laura which concludes—

And this is what dull fools have named to die,
Upon her fair face death itself seemed fair.

—came from the depths of her heart: *she* loved Laura too.

Emma was thirty-six years old when she first saw Italy, but in mind and spirit she was older still. At the same time, however, she trembled like a child for joy. In her childhood reveries about Portugal, of which she later told William Morris, Emma had asked her father, "Are there mules there? Are there vineyards?" Now she experienced for the first time what a hundred thousand painters had seen:

> Veder le cose belle
> Que portan il ciel.

Light that seemed to fall through a glass of clear wine. And the air, the ethereal air, the divine intoxication of air of which she had once written in *Alide*: "Do you not feel this mountain air tingling like wine through your veins? My blood is all aglow within me—my heart is as light as a flame."

What a miracle, to be able to live in a land that since early youth she had really thought a dream—although she had learned the language and had a wonderful command of it.

> To kneel upon the ground where Dante trod,
> To breathe the air of immortality
> From Angelo and Raphael—*to be*—
> Each sense new-quickened by a demi-god.

Salvini was not in Florence in December when she called upon him. But after all, what did it matter? "To hear the liquid Tuscan speech at whiles from citizen to peasant. . . ." More than that the greatest actor could not give her.

Pisa, Florence, the countryside between these cities. "Each tower, castle and village shining like a jewel; the olive, the fig, and at your feet the roses, growing in mid-December." And at last—Rome.

40

Rome, as Goethe once remarked, is not Italy: it is more. Years ago Emma herself had described, very realistically, the experience of a man who nears Rome:

> He trudged amidst the sea of poisonous flowers
> On the Campagna's undulating plain,
> With Rome, the many-steepled, many-towered,
> Before him, regnant on her throne of hills.
> A thick blue cloud of haze o'erhung the town,
> But the fast-sinking sun struck fiery light
> From shining crosses, roofs, and flashing domes.
> Across his path an arching bridge of stone
> Was raised above a shrunken yellow stream,
> Hurrying with the light on every wave
> Towards the great town and outward to the sea.
> Upon the bridge's crest he paused, and leaned
> Against the barrier, throwing back his cowl,
> And gazed upon the dull, unlovely flood
> That was the Tiber. Quaggy banks lay bare,
> Muddy and miry, glittering in the sun,
> And myriad insects hovered o'er the reeds,
> Whose lithe, moist tips by listless airs were stirred.
> When the low sun had dropped behind the hills,
> He found himself within the streets of Rome,
> Walking as in a sleep, where naught seemed real.

But the landscape of these verses, written in May 1870, had been seen through the eyes of Tannhäuser, the unhappy knight whose heart was torn between the pagan Venus and the Christian Elisabeth: "Pagan through mind and Christian through the heart." When Emma approached Rome sixteen years later there was no such strife in her heart. As her sister Josephine assures us, "true to her old attractions" *pagan* Rome appealed to her most strongly—stronger in any case than the Rome of the popes and the Middle Ages.

Truly, she rejoiced in St. Peter's dome and the other majestic witnesses of the Age of Faith; but it was the Rome of antiquity and the Greek statuary of the Vatican and Capitoline museums that was responsible for "wiping out all other places and impressions, and opening a whole new world of sensations." So in a moment she forgot her new love, painting, and was wholly taken up with sculpture: "I am even out of humor with pictures; a bit of broken stone or a fragment of a bas-relief, or a Corinthian column standing out against this lapis-lazuli sky, or a tremendous arch, are the only things I can look at for the moment,—except the Sistine Chapel, which is as gigantic as the rest, and forces itself upon you with equal might."

The secret of Emma's apparent indifference to Christian ideas is to be found in her classical, almost Stoical, conception of death. She was not in love with death; but she hated it as little as she believed in the existence of a heaven to be won by faith. It was only that she was continually preoccupied by the fact of its existence on this earth. In the midst of the beauties of Rome she writes to Josephine: "I have to exert all my strength not to lose myself in morbidness and depression." For these mixed reasons her feelings were drawn to a modern spot in Rome that was at the same time very old, the place where Shelley and Keats lie buried.

Emma knew the legendary story of their life and death very well. When the drowned corpse of Shelley was washed ashore near Leghorn in 1822, Italian law required that it be immediately burned on the spot. So Byron and a few other friends sprinkled oil, salt, wine and incense on the body and set it afire; but, strangely enough, though everything else was burned to ashes, the poet's heart would not catch fire. George Trelawney, one of the friends, reached into the fire, burning his own hand, and snatched Shelley's heart from the flames.

When Shelley drowned, there was a volume of poetry in his coat pocket written by another pagan—Keats. Keats at that time had been dead two years. He had been snatched away by tuberculosis at a time when the poet in him had been completely realized, but the man had only first begun to live. He had closely watched his illness: "He saw all of it," as his friend, Joseph Severn, wrote, "and his knowledge of anatomy made it tenfold worse at every change." Shelley, in comparison, had died an almost happy man in a shipwreck on a July morning, not knowing that he had to die. Now Shelley lay in the Protestant cemetery in Rome, in the shadow of the pyramid of Caius Cestius, in a niche formed by two buttresses of the old Roman wall; his otherwise blank stone is adorned by three lines from Shakespeare's *Tempest*. Emma visited the graves of Shelley and Keats very often, although (as Parnes learned from members of the American colony in Rome) they were a long distance away from her hotel. There she stood "in her deep modesty, though with an almost sisterly feeling," and softly repeated what Prospero had said of life and death:

> We are such stuff
> As dreams are made on, and our little life
> Is rounded with a sleep.

"It is all heart-breaking," Emma writes in the presence of the graves. But they seem to her to be symbols of the past in general, and she writes further: "I don't only mean those beautiful graves overgrown with acanthus and violets, but the mutilated arches and columns and dumb appealing fragments looming up in the glowing sunshine under the Roman blue sky." The only reality which had the might to lure her from the "graves of the past" was the Roman spring. Yes, by February the air was already pregnant with spring. The grass of the orchards shone in an unbelievably deep green. Violets were out and the rosy snow of the almond blossoms. From the bottom of her heart she cried out: "Oh! The divine, the celestial, the unheard-of beauty of it all!"

41

By June she was back in England. She spent the whole summer there, not so much in London as in Herefordshire, possibly with Browning and his sister. Here she was visited, among others, by young Parnes who found her "buried up to both ears in all the English and American periodicals she had missed in Italy." The youth, at that time an ardent advocate of socialism, engaged her in a long controversy about Henry George and his agrarian socialism (he knew her sonnet, "Progress and Poverty," published four years earlier in the *New York Times*) and admired how well versed she, the poetess, was even in details. "There's small wonder!" she remarked. "After reading carefully the land laws of the Old Testament everybody should know what the American agrarian reformers think and why they think it!" Her unusual seriousness made a deep impression on the young man. It seemed impossible for her to utter banal or casual remarks about the common things of life. She was exactly in the mood in which, a few years earlier, Constance Harrison had seen her, when Emma had visited her at her home in Lenox, Massachusetts: "Sometimes in our drives talk became so earnest that we would find ourselves halted in some grassy wayside nook, the mare's head bent down to crop rich clover, when we discussed points of mutual interest. . . ."

In the Malvern Hills, too, Emma loved to walk through the countryside. There Elizabeth Barrett's father had built his mansion. There, where

. . . the ground's most gentle dimplement
(As if God's finger touched but did not press
In making England)

had charmed the child, amidst the "up and down of verdure," Elizabeth once had had a frightening experience: she had seen (and wonderfully described later) a magnificent tree blasted and consumed by lightning. A tree was certainly a living being, and to see this majestic giant tree burned to ashes before her own eyes had left a deep impression on her.

At that same spot, ominously named "Hope End," Emma Lazarus was attacked by a mysterious disease. When she fell ill this second time, it did not seem to be the same illness she had suffered from the year before in America. "A jolt passed through her body," a nameless shock. It was not tuberculosis, not articular rheumatism. She suffered pain, now in one part of her body, now in another. Soon swallowing became difficult for her and her digestion was impaired. But at the beginning the mental effects were worse than the physical. "She was oppressed by a languor and heaviness amounting almost to lethargy." To overcome the leaden feeling of her mind and body, she got up out of bed once more and went to Holland, and there felt so deceptively healthy that she began to lay the foundations of a book on Rembrandt. Joyous and dreaming of Italy, she arrived in Paris again. Paris was to be only a way station; in December she planned to return to the lovely, beloved Mediterranean and to visit Florence and Rome for a second time. Nothing but this projected journey was of interest to her. In an English newspaper she read that President Grover

Cleveland had unveiled the Statue of Liberty on October 28, 1886, but the item left her cold; it was all so strange and remote, as though it were not her statue, as well.

Then the disease launched a fearful blow and threw her to her knees. In Heine's Paris, in the Paris where Heine had lain on his "mattress grave," Emma Lazarus fell deathly sick. Was it really the horrible disease whose very name spells death? The disease that begins by being the size of a pinhead and often takes years to grow large as a pea; in which pain makes its first appearance when it is really too late, when the cancer has already reached the nerves. Was it really cancer? After all, Emma was in Paris where, following the great Récamier, the best cancer diagnosticians of the time then lived. How careless of her that she did not go to see any of them. It was almost as if shame held her back. Thomas Mann observes in *The Magic Mountain* that disease is an immoral condition, the rebellion of the body against the mind. If that is true, there is no disease more immoral than cancer. It is not even caused by a germ; it arises in the body itself, the result of a wholly illogical and uncontrolled growth of cells. It is the "laughter of death" at the divinely planned form of the body.

"Woman's body is a poem written by the Lord God himself," Heinrich Heine once wrote. That womanly beauty surpassed by far the canon of man's beauty was an axiom long held to by Emma. In an earlier series of poems ("Symphonic Studies," after Robert Schumann) she had expressed this conviction in Keatsian fashion:

What do the sea-nymphs in that coral cave?
   With wondering eyes their supple forms they bend
   O'er something rarely beautiful. They lend
Their lithe white arms, and through the golden wave
They lift it tenderly. Oh blinding sight!

    A naked, radiant goddess, tranced in sleep,
    Full-limbed, voluptuous, 'neath the mantling sweep
Of auburn locks that kiss her ankles white!
Upward they bear her, chanting low and sweet:
    The clinging waters part before their way,
Jewels of flame are dancing 'neath their feet.
    Up in the sunshine, on soft foam, they lay
Their precious burden, and return forlorn.
Oh, bliss! oh, anguish! Mortals, *Love* is born!

The only mistake Emma had apparently made in these verses was to link Botticelli's "Birth of Venus" with Robert Schumann's *Symphonische Etüden*. Schumann, in that manliest and most energetic of his piano works, had probably seen hunters breaking through the underbrush of a Rhine forest, but never the birth of Venus out of a classical Mediterranean seascape. Be this as it may, it was the Venus type, the woman of spotless beauty, that Emma had adored her whole life through. And now she was menaced, no, already attacked by a dreadful, disfiguring disease. It began, in all probability, with grotesque glandular swellings beneath the ear, around the neck and in the axillae. The malady from which she suffered, like all cancer-like diseases, could be treated by X-ray in its primary stages. But it still lacked a few years until Wilhelm Konrad Roentgen was to make his great discovery and Emma Lazarus could only be treated by large doses of arsenic (*tinctura fowleri*)—a means that was never able to prevent the infection from spreading to the mediastinum and the abdomen.

    One day, driven by her seemingly inexhaustible will and scoffing at her pains, Emma left her bed and dressed. Yearning again for *cose belle*, to "drink them in with the eyes" for the last time, the mortally ill woman tottered to the Louvre where, four decades before, Heine had suffered and the Venus of Milo had lacked the arms to gather him to her healing bosom. A few years before she had written her "Venus of the Louvre":

> Down the long hall she glistens like a star,
> The foam-born mother of Love, transfixed to stone,
> Yet none the less immortal, breathing on.
> Time's brutal hand hath maimed but could not mar.
> When first the enthralled enchantress from afar
> Dazzled mine eyes, I saw her not alone,
> Serenely poised on her world-worshipped throne,
> As when she guided once her dove-drawn car,—
> But at her feet a pale, death-stricken Jew,
> Her life adorer, sobbed farewell to love.
> Here *Heine* wept! Here still he weeps anew,
> Nor ever shall his shadow lift or move,
> While mourns one ardent heart, one poet-brain
> For vanished Hellas and Hebraic pain.

When she returned home "with ashen-gray brow, bathed in perspiration, a tragic priestess with the eyes of a Sappho," she knew that she would never again see Italy and life. At the height of her illness one of her sisters came to Paris to stay by her bedside. But Emma felt alone. In spite of sisterly hands, she lay alone, terribly alone in an utterly strange city. She had ample time to experience the truth of Goethe's lines:

> Wer sich der Einsamkeit ergibt
> Ach, der ist bald allein.

There was only enough strength remaining to her to pack her belongings, with the help of her sister and a good-natured hotel maid, and to take ship for New York. This was dangerous, but, as Josephine later said, it had to be done. And what was Emma's goal in this? To return to America to die. . . .

Why did she not choose to die in Italy? A few years after her death Robert Browning was to die in the Palazzo Rezzonico, on whose walls is that inscription every Venetian knows:

> Open my heart and you will see
> Graven inside of it: ITALY.

But no, Emma Lazarus had to go back to New York to die.

42

It has often been alleged that, once she had been visited by illness and pain, Emma's interest in the Jewish cause abated. This is not true at all. Emma was already ill when she wrote her cycle of lyrics, "By the Waters of Babylon."

In this remarkable series of poems, which *The Century Magazine* published in March 1887—half a year before her death, that is—we see once more, compressed into a narrow space, all the themes, poetical, historical, cultural and political, that for Emma Lazarus made up the "Jewish reality and the Jewish dream." The first poem is "The Exodus," a description of what took place on August 3, 1492. Again and again, in verse and in prose, Emma had described these things. Now she did it for the last time. As if she herself were taking leave of this scene:

> The Spanish noon is a blaze of azure fire, and the dusty pilgrims crawl like an endless serpent along treeless plains and bleached high-roads, through rock-split ravines and castellated, cathedral-shadowed towns.
>
> The hoary patriarch, wrinkled as an almond shell, bows painfully upon his staff. The beautiful young mother, ivory-pale, well-nigh swoons beneath her burden; in her large enfolding arms nestles her sleeping babe, round her knees flock her little ones with bruised and bleeding feet. "Mother, shall we soon be there?"

The youth with Christ-like countenance speaks comfortably to father and brother, to maiden and wife. In his breast, his own heart is broken.

The halt, the blind, are amid the train. Sturdy pack-horses laboriously drag the tented wagons wherein lie the sick athirst with fever.

The panting mules are urged forward with spur and goad; stuffed are the heavy saddle-bags with the wreckage of ruined homes.

Hark to the tinkling silver bells that adorn the tenderly carried silken scrolls.

In the fierce noon-glare a lad bears a kindled lamp; behind its network of bronze the airs of heaven breathe not upon its faint purple star.

Noble and abject, learned and simple, illustrious and obscure, plod side by side, all brothers now, all merged in one routed army of misfortune.

Woe to the straggler who falls by the wayside! No friend shall close his eyes.

They leave behind, the grape, the olive, and the fig; the vines they planted, the corn they sowed, the garden-cities of Andalusia and Aragon, Estremadura and La Mancha, of Granada and Castile; the altar, the hearth, and the grave of their fathers.

The townsman spits at their garments, the shepherd quits his flock, the peasant his plow, to pelt with curses and stones; the villager sets on their trail his yelping cur.

Oh the weary march, oh the uptorn roots of home, oh the blankness of the receding goal!

Listen to their lamentation: *They that ate dainty food are desolate in the streets; they that were reared in scarlet embrace dung-hills. They flee away and wander about. Men say among the nations, they shall no more sojourn there; our end is near, our days are full, our doom is come.*

Whither shall they turn? for the West hath cast them out, and the East refuseth to receive.

Oh bird of the air, whisper to the despairing exiles, that to-day, to-day, from the many-masted, gayly-bannered port of Palos, sails the world-unveiling Genoese, to unlock the golden gates of sunset and bequeath a Continent to Freedom!

Another poem, "Currents," is compacted of certain notions and visions that had preoccupied Emma since 1881. The train of her thought leads her from the czarist pogroms to the Statue of Liberty. But this poem lacks the clarity of the foregoing one; there is a fogginess about it, and it has been composed with the haste of a person who no longer has much time to lose:

Vast oceanic movements, the flux and reflux of immeasurable tides oversweep our continent.

From the far Caucasian steppes, from the squalid Ghettos of Europe,

From Odessa and Bucharest, from Kief and Ekaterinoslav,

Hark to the cry of the exiles of Babylon, the voice of Rachel mourning for her children, of Israel lamenting for Zion.

And lo, like a turbid stream, the long-pent flood bursts the dykes of oppression and rushes hitherward.

Unto her ample breast, the generous mother of nations welcomes them.

The herdsman of Canaan and the seed of Jerusalem's royal shepherd renew their youth amid the pastoral plains of Texas and the golden valleys of the Sierras.

There is ample evidence that Emma, when she wrote these poems, had known Walt Whitman's *Leaves of Grass* for twenty years at least, and it is equally certain that she had no real liking for Whitman's form despite the respect in which she held his *Democratic Vistas* because of its "divine mixture of poetry and politics." The cause for this can be easily guessed. Even after the *Parnassus* incident, and in spite of her having later complained that Emerson's lyrics lacked the essential spontaneity of that form, she long remained under the spell of Emerson's aesthetic; and Emerson's own attitude to Whitman did not fail to exercise an influence on her.

Emerson's attitude to Whitman passed through several stages. (Edmund Wilson has recently listed them.) There is little doubt that Emerson was the earliest American fully to appreciate the great significance of Whitman. But later he grew testy when Whitman refused to remove some lines that Emerson considered improper from a second edition of his poems. For hours Emerson vainly pleaded with him to make his book "readable for honest people."

Generally, however, Emerson's attitude to Whitman was one of good-natured tolerance, mixed with some criticism; John Burroughs, in his journal entry of December 21, 1871, reports the following: " 'Yes,' Emerson said in a very gay mood, 'Walt sends me all his books. But tell Walt, I am not satisfied—not satisfied. I expect him to make the songs of the Nation—but he seems to be contented to—make the *inventories.*' " Emma Lazarus, who after all was half a Victorian poetess, could hardly feel otherwise; Whitman's interminable lines, his endless catalogues, for years must have seemed utterly foreign, even repellent to her. To see her now—just six months before her death!—fall helplessly under the spell of the great example of Whitman, is almost shocking.

For the first and last time Emma Lazarus made use of that distinctive feature of Walt Whitman's style, the long line, and she did it without restriction. The basis of Whitman's long line, of his "Appalachian largeness," as Van Wyck Brooks terms it, was Whitman's bursting good health, and, above all, his omnivorous interest in all of life. Whitman's great vigor and dynamism—Lincoln, in 1862, when he saw Whitman passing by "in worker's sleeves," had involuntarily remarked: "There goes a man"—were of course utterly lacking in the dark-haired, ephebic Emma, with her thin scholar's body. On her the great Whitman line hung as loosely and awkwardly as a sack. We can dismiss "By the Waters of Babylon" as the failing effort of a failing spirit. It was a despairing attempt, while the breath still lasted in her, to express as much as she possibly could. Seen in this light, her resorting to the Whitmanesque "inventory," her cramming everything together in ragged, running lines, does not seem so unnatural. It is very moving, rather, in the last Jewish poem Emma wrote, "The Prophet," to read these lines:

Moses Ben Maimon lifting his perpetual lamp over the path of the perplexed;
Hallevi, the honey-tongued poet, wakening amid the silent ruins of Zion the sleeping lyre of David;
Moses, the wise son of Mendel, who made the Ghetto illustrious;
Abarbanel, the counselor of kings; Alcharisi, the exquisite singer; Ibn Ezra, the perfect old man; Gabirol, the tragic seer;
Heine, the enchanted magician, the heart-broken jester;
Yea, and the century-crowned patriarch whose bounty engirdles the globe;—

These need no wreath and no trumpet; like perennial asphodel blossoms, their fame, their glory resounds like the brazen-throated cornet.

But thou—hast thou faith in the fortune of Israel? Wouldst thou lighten the anguish of Jacob?

Then shalt thou take the hand of yonder caftaned wretch with flowing curls and gold-pierced ears;

Who crawls blinking forth from the loathsome recesses of the Jewry;

Nerveless his fingers, puny his frame; haunted by the batlike phantoms of superstition is his brain.

Thou shalt say to the bigot, "My Brother," and to the creature of darkness, "My Friend,".

And thy heart shall spend itself in fountains of love upon the ignorant, the coarse, and the abject.

Then in the obscurity thou shalt hear a rush of wings, thine eyes shall be bitten with pungent smoke.

And close against thy quivering lips shall be pressed the live coal wherewith the Seraphim brand the Prophets.

Walt Whitman, of course, did not know of those "poems in prose," none of which could have been written without his example. (He knew, and liked, some of her earlier poems.) But he seemed to have been sensitive to more things in her than were other persons who knew her better.

With his flair for personality (unsurpassed by any of his contemporaries) he spoke after Emma's death of her "great, sweet, unusual nature." And then he added, somewhat plaintively: "I never met her—several times came near doing so. It may be gratuitous to say so—no doubt is —but I have randomly, wholly at random, believed she did not wish to meet me—rather avoided me. . . . I have had reasons for feeling its truth—good reasons, though reasons rather emotional than concrete. If she did deliberately set about not to see me she was put up to it."

Horace Traubel, whose *Walt Whitman in Camden* is the source for this remark, makes no comment on it. Albert Mordell has recently written that Whitman's belief that Emma Lazarus shunned him was a "misapprehension." But why a misapprehension? As much as we dislike seeing Emma involved in that silly New England conspiracy to make the great poet a social outcast, "on account of his hobo-like manners," it is very possible that this was the case. The conspiracy was a large one. Lidian Emerson for decades shut her house to Walt Whitman. Emma was, as Constance Harrison later described her, "the most feminine woman," and she may have feared and felt a distaste for Whitman.

On the other hand, "that rowdy," as James Russell Lowell used to speak of Whitman, had a keen sense for tenderness in women. Speaking of Emma Lazarus—although he had never seen her—he said: "She was . . . quite different from the great body of professional women." And comparing her to Agnes Repplier, whose last book, *Men and Things*, must have irked him, he said: "There was nothing vitriolic in Emma Lazarus' work!"

43

New York Harbor flamed with the midsummer sun of 1887. Emma's despairing family came to the pier to meet a dying woman. Thereafter Emma did not leave her bed and saw scarcely anyone save Josephine, her favorite sister. She may have permitted Richard Gilder to see her, for a few minutes; a sonnet of his speaks of her as "writhing on her bed of pain." In general, however, Emma preferred to shut herself away from the world completely rather than to expose her physical disfigurement to others.

In the excellent sketch of Heine's life with which she had prefaced her *Poems and Ballads of Heinrich Heine*, she had written: "No word of complaint or impatience ever passed his lips; on the contrary, with his old, irresistible humor, his fancy played about his own privations and sufferings, and tried to alleviate for his devoted wife and friends the pain of the heart-rending spectacle. His delicate consideration prompted him to spare his venerable mother all knowledge of his illness. He wrote to her every month in his customary cheerful way; and, in sending her the latest volumes of his poetry, he caused a separate copy always to be printed, from which all allusions to his malady were expunged. 'For that matter,' he said, 'that any son could be as wretched and miserable as I, no mother would believe.' "

Take away the "irresistible humor" and the case of Heine is the case of Emma Lazarus, who did not want anyone to see how sick she was. However, Josephine and Sarah could not be fooled; even without a pronouncement from the doctor, they knew that their favorite sister was lost to them. With great emotion Josephine noted that, between attacks of raging pain and submergence in seas of opium, Emma appeared, though but a shadow of herself, "kindled, full of a wonderful fire, even brilliant."

Emma lived in what was now Sarah's home: 18 West Tenth Street. What did these sisters speak about? We do not know exactly; but the talk might have been, among other things, of Heine perhaps. Now six years before Emma had made this observation in her Heine essay: "During the long sleepless night when he lay writhing with pain or exhausted by previous paroxysms, his mind, preternaturally clear and vigorous, conceived the glowing fantasies of the *Romancero*, or the Job-like lamentations of the *Lazarus* poems." Lazarus! Emma was well aware of what the name of Lazarus signified. It was a Greek name derived from the Hebrew Eleazar, which means "God has helped"—it is the name of that man in the New Testament who is raised from the dead by a miracle.

Even at the time when she had appeared in the best of health, Emma had quoted, as a rather melancholy joke, the German nursery rhyme:

> Ich bin der arme Lazarus,
> Der still zu Bette liegen muss.

Alas—now it was all too true, she was poor Lazarus, painfully prostrated on his bed, and no miracle could save her.

But, unlike Heine, she did not indulge in "Job-like lamentations"; no, this "mortally ill Jewess," this "emaciated picture of woe," in her last days flew back in spirit to Italy. It was beauty she longed for; that beauty of which Shelley had said, in lines that Emma had always cherished: "Poetry redeems from decay the visitations of the divinity in man. Poetry turns all things to loveliness; it exalts the beauty of that which is most beautiful, and it adds beauty to that which is most deformed; . . ." Yes, deformed—and against the "deformation" of her own self by a merciless and a senseless disease, she protested with the last breath of her life.

Even on her deathbed she wrote pagan philosophical poetry expressing her worship of beauty. Max Baym is doubtless right in believing that the last poem she wrote was her translation of Carducci's *In Una Chiesa Gotica* ("In a Gothic Church"), which is itself an unmistakable declaration against the "worship of suffering":

In slender, longdrawn vistas they arise,
The tall, unmoving, marble stems
And in the sacred gloom they seem to me,
A giant's army, meditating war
With the invisible.

. . . .

I seek not God among you, marble stems,
Aerial arches. Trembling I await
The sound of that familiar little foot
Which faintly will awake your solemn echoes.

'Tis Lydia and she turns—slow as she turns,
Her lustrous locks define her face for me,
Love on the pallid visage briefly smiles
From out that veil of black.

Thus in a Gothic temple's doubtful light,
Once waited Alighieri tremblingly—
Seeking God's image in the gemlike pallor
Of a fair woman.

Beneath the snowy veil, her virgin brow
Limpid shone forth, arrayed in ecstasy,
Whilst among clouds of fervid incense smoke
Mounted the litany.

Mounted with murmurs soft, with quivering breath,
Joyously mounted like a flock of doves.
Again, as with the sobs of myriad woes,
Imploring help from heaven.

Athwart the hollow space the organ sent
Sighing and shuddering towards the ringing vault.
It seemed as if the souls of buried friends
Beneath the earth responded.

But from the mythic heights of Fiesole
Through rosy glass, blazoned with pious tales,

Apollo gazed, and on the tall high altar
Waved the dim tapers.

And Dante saw amongst the angelic hymns,
The Tuscan virgin apotheosized—
And heard beneath his footsteps, groan the dragons
Of the Inferno.

But I see neither angel choirs nor friends,
I see a feeble light fall tremulous
Through the damp air, and a cold twilight seizes
The languid spirit.

. . . .

It is at this point that the poet Carducci bids farewell to a God in whose doctrines and service *continua . . . la morte domina* ("death perpetually dominates"). And with a trembling hand the translator tried to finish the poem:

Oh inaccessible Lord of souls, thy temples
Exclude the living sunshine!
Thou, martyr crucified, dost crucify!
Contaminating all the air with sadness. . . .

And, going on with the original:

*ma i cieli splendono, ma i campi ridono
ma d'amore lampeggiano
gli occhi di Lidia. . . .*

in a well-nigh illegible hand Emma put down her hymnlike translation, like a eulogy of life itself: "Meanwhile the heavens glow, the meadows laugh, / Meanwhile with love refulgent shine Lydia's eyes." When she reached the climax of these lines—"shine Lydia's eyes"—the light went out of Emma's own eyes. Art and life died together.

Gustav Gottheil stood at her bier. (She had long since obliged him and contributed to his prayer book.) But there were not too many people who stood by her bier on November 20, 1887—certainly John Greenleaf Whittier overrated Emma Lazarus' place in the public eye when, overcome by a noble feeling of sorrow, this poet, himself a warrior of the Spirit, wrote to the *American Hebrew*: "The announcement of the death of one who has gained an honorable place in our literature has been read by both Jew and Christian with a sorrow which is almost universal. Her songs of the Divine Unity repeated on the lips of her own people in all zones and continents, have been heard round the world. With no lack of rhythmic sweetness, she has often the rugged strength and verbal audacity of Browning. Since Miriam sang of deliverance and triumph by the Red Sea, the Semitic race has had no braver singer. 'The Crowing of the Red Cock,' written when the Russian sky was red with blazing Hebrew horror, is an indignant and forceful lyric worthy of the Maccabean age. Her 'Banner of the Jew' has the ring of Israel's war trumpet. Well may those of her own race and faith lament the loss of such a woman. They will not sorrow alone. Among the 'mourning women' at her grave, the sympathizing voice of Christian daughters will mingle with the wail of the daughters of Jerusalem." This high tribute was published by *The American Hebrew*, in a special issue dedicated to Emma's memory, and put out a few weeks after her death. It contained contributions by other men of letters—Robert Browning, of course, among them. To this issue and to a later one, Stedman, Eggleston and John Hays, too, contributed. Even Harriet Beecher Stowe, whose *Uncle Tom's Cabin* was the most widely read American book, wrote a few words of farewell to one of her less popular sisters. For a while Brentano's, Dillingham's and other book shops sold the few remaining copies of *Songs of a Semite*. And then a curtain of impenetrable darkness fell around Emma Lazarus.

44

"Much mystery surrounded . . . the death of Miss Lazarus," Philip Cowen wrote much later in his excellent *Memories of an American Jew*. What was the mystery? Some persons thought that only a suicide could have departed this life with such sinister swiftness. On July 31 she had arrived in New York; by November 19 she was dead. But at the time people did not know how swiftly cancer can strike after it has long played its perverse cat-and-mouse game with the body. Moreover Emma had closed the doors against almost everybody. Not until her death did many people learn that she had returned from abroad.

The shock and dismay that overcame the Jewish community when they learned of the wholly unexpected death of one of their most distinguished members was so great that one of Emma's sisters had to hurry up to the old Portuguese synagogue (Congregation Shearith Israel) on West Nineteenth Street, of which the Lazarus family were members, in order to dictate into the sexton's book that Emma had succumbed to "Hodgkin's Disease" (the particular type of cancer Emma had suffered from). This was in itself an unusual thing to do; one can leaf through fifty pages of the synagogue book and not find one instance where the cause of death is given.

But there is indisputable proof that Emma did really die of a cancerous disease: not only the death certificate, written out by a Dr. E. L. Partridge, but also the testimony of Emma's friend, Rose Hawthorne Lathrop, the daughter of Nathaniel Hawthorne. ("This young woman of finest promise and exalted perception died in her prime of cancer.") Not only was Rose Hawthorne one of the last persons to see Emma, but she was also so profoundly moved by Emma's death and the sufferings that had preceded it that she changed her entire way of life. She became a nun and worked as a nurse in the Lower East Side slums, where (under the name of Mother Alphonsa) she tried to help not only those incurables who were stricken with cancer but also those who were stricken with poverty.

The mystery is not in her death, but in what happened *after* Emma Lazarus died.

The complete oblivion into which she fell is not merely inexplicable; there is something contrived about it. Where are Emma's diaries? Where are her original manuscripts? Where is her extensive library, which included books in six languages, theology, philosophy, ethnology, literature and history?

We can only guess what happened. During the confusions of the Dreyfus decade (which not only rent France, but split the entire cultural world into two camps), Emma's heritage was dissipated in the conflict between two sisters, one of whom stood in the Dreyfus camp and the other in the anti-Dreyfus camp. Emma's *spiritual* heir was, of course, her faithful sister Josephine, who not only cherished the Jewish tradition, but contributed to it in her own right. Josephine's book, *The Spirit of Judaism* (1895), is a noble book, its formulations of a classical purity. Emma must have been looking over her sister's shoulder when Josephine sat down and expressed ideas such as these: "Judaism in its actuality, in its very constitution, as we know it to-day, as we have known it through all time . . . is the religion of particularism, the religion of a particular people, chosen and set apart. . . . But Judaism in its ultimate destiny, in its essence and its spirit, is a universal religion—the religion of humanity when humanity shall have grown to its full stature, the religion of the world when the world shall be capable of grasping and realizing its lofty ideals." This surely was spirit of Emma's spirit.

But unquestionably the youngest sister, Annie, possessed far more information about Emma and far more material from Emma's own hand, because of their travels together. Strangely enough, Annie also held the copyright to Emma's writings; at first she shared it with Mary, who was not interested in literature and who, later, when she married and moved to Germany, surrendered all her rights to Annie. In 1899 Josephine wrote a book on Lucie Dreyfus, the martyred captain's wife. In this book (*Madame Dreyfus*) she lauded Lucie Dreyfus as an example for all women.

It must have been because of this book that the final break occurred. Apparently Annie could not stand reading passages like the following: "It has been foolishly disputed who is the hero of the Dreyfus affair, because, strangely enough, that strange and evil machination of the darkness has had its luminous side, has brought forth more than one creature of the light, more than one magnificent heroic personality." (Josephine, of course, here refers to Emile Zola and Colonel Picquart.) Then she continues: "But there can be no doubt as to the heroine. Madame Dreyfus stands alone, crowned with the crown of perfect womanhood, with that halo of perfect love which makes grief beautiful. . . . France may still be proud that a woman like Madame Dreyfus was born in her midst. But Madame Dreyfus does not belong to France alone, although she be a Frenchwoman; she does not belong to Judaism, though she be a Jewess. She belongs to the world, and to all mankind and womankind for all time, because she is the type of woman before whom the world must ever bow, possessing as she does that quality which is the right divine of all women—the genius, the gift of loving."

We do not know whether Annie Lazarus really believed in the guilt of the poor French captain—that he had betrayed his country—but, in any case, to defend him was an act of "Jewish self-advertising" to this peculiar daughter of Moses Lazarus. Josephine may have retorted sharply—and the result was a total break between the two sisters.

Annie Lazarus, whose name after her marriage was Annie Humphrey Johnstone, moved to Rome, later to Venice, and became an ardent Catholic. Emma, who was otherwise quite without prejudice in her association with people of all creeds, had hated converts. "We should prove," she had once written to Cowen, "to Christian missionaries that 'converted Jews' are probably not only the most expensive of all marketable commodities but also the most worthless after they are purchased." Annie took her revenge by writing from Italy to forbid the printing of "anything Jewish" in any new edition of Emma's works.

This strange act, which was reported by Philip Cowen and has been much commented on since, actually took place in a pleasanter and more diplomatic form, we now know; for the letter has recently been found. It was sent from the Palazzo Contarini, Venice, and is dated February 25, 1926. It is addressed to Bernard G. Richards of New York, a well-known publicist who had served in 1919 as Secretary of the American Jewish Delegation to the Versailles Peace Conference. In the middle of the twenties Richards was engaged in a publishing venture of his own and had put out works by Georges Clemenceau, Stefan Zweig, Korolenko, Georg Brandes and Leon Kobrin, most of which had Jewish themes. To this list Richards wished to add the complete works of Emma Lazarus.

To Richards' inquiry Annie Lazarus answered that great difficulties stood in the way of the project. She did have the copper plates used for the original edition put out by Houghton, Mifflin—"I hold them intact, always having hoped that an occasion would present itself when they might be used"—but, she continues, "when the question comes up of issuing a new edition, with all the necessity of advertising involved thereby, fresh problems arise. I now realize to the full how great a change has taken place during the interval of years that have elapsed since these volumes first made their appearance.

"My sister would have been the first, I feel sure, to recognize this. Events of forty years back are neither present actualities nor yet remote enough to be judged as history. And while her politico-religious poems are technically as fine as anything she ever wrote, they were nevertheless composed in a moment of emotional excitement, which would seem to make their theme of questionable appropriateness today; in fact, to me, it seems out of harmony with the spirit of the present time.

"There has been, moreover, a tendency, I think, on the part of some of her public, to overemphasize the Hebraic strain of her work, giving it thus a quality of sectarian propaganda, which I greatly deplore, for I understood this to have been merely a phase in my sister's development, called forth by righteous indignation at the tragic happenings of those days. Then, unfortunately, owing to her untimely death, this was destined to be her final word."

Out of harmony with the spirit of the present time? Even within the walls of a Venetian palazzo Annie Lazarus could not have failed to perceive how the dirty waters of anti-Semitism were rising in Central and Eastern Europe in the year 1926, and how it threatened to engulf the people of whom after all she was so close a part. For Annie was not only the daughter of Moses Lazarus, she was, on her mother's side, a descendant of Rabbi Gershom Seixas, the ardent patriot of the American Revolution who had presided over New York's Shearith Israel Congregation for fifty years. But no! The Jewish awakening of Emma Lazarus had been, in her sister's mind, only an *episode*. Merely a phase in her development, understandable, but somewhat unfortunate, too. All that Emma had stood for in the last seven years of her life merely a phase! The Russian pogroms, Wards Island and Palestine, a phase. Even the last four lines of her poem "The New Ezekiel":

>The spirit is not dead, proclaim the word.
>Where lay dead bones a host of armed men stand!
>I ope your graves, my people, saith the Lord,
>And I shall place you living in your land.

A phase—Annie Lazarus, with the diplomacy of a *grande dame*, continued to write: "If my sister were here today I feel that she might prefer to be remembered by the verses written in her more serene mood" (!). And then she submitted, very politely, a list of "a very beautiful small selection of her verses"—thirty poems in all, and nothing, of course, that had the remotest connection with the Hebraic spirit or the Jewish cause. So Richards had to renounce his wish to reprint the complete works of Emma Lazarus.

Such are the facts. And we are probably justified in deducing from these and other facts that not only the copper plates, but also a good many unprinted manuscripts, diaries and letters could have been in the possession of Annie Lazarus-Johnstone when she died a few years ago. Precious material that would enable us to fill in so many lacunae in Emma's personal and intellectual development. But where is it now, the material? Where is the hidden chest, if it still exists?

Emma, too, is to blame for our knowing so little about her. She concealed the simplest facts concerning her own person; she drew the line between her private life and her public activities or writing much more sternly than most reputable people would do. Her face was by no means unattractive, because of its characteristic alternations of expression; and Walt Whitman was most struck by it when he saw it, engraved by Johnson, in the *Century*, issue of October 1888. Constance Harrison, speaking on a certain occasion of that swiftly changing face of hers, remarked that it was first "mutinous and inclined to be sarcastic," but then "her brow cleared, her eye lightened, she became gentle and tender in a moment." But this face—of which Parnes even fifty years later spoke as a "forest densely populated with thoughts"—she was so little fond of, that it would appear she had no photographs taken, or at least never gave any to her friends. (In 1878 the Berlin writer, Rudolf Lindau, apparently pleaded in vain to get one.) When anyone of her acquaintances thought he was on the point of gaining a more intimate knowledge of her, she drew back with virginal bashfulness. As a result, our knowledge of her has been pretty well limited for a long time to the loving sketch that Josephine, a year after her sister's death, wrote for the *Century* and later appended to *The Poems of Emma Lazarus* (1889). With the publication of the two volumes of these *Poems*, which were never reissued (and which contained many bad poems and omitted many good ones), Emma was buried and forgotten. Now and then some literary friend of hers, such as Edmund Clarence Stedman, wrote an essay on the quiet poet (in *Genius and Other Essays*) or, correcting Emerson's mistake, put her in an anthology of poetry. In 1905 Richard Watson Gilder, her friend of earlier days, wrote a sonnet on the forgotten poetess. And that was all. And for sustaining fame it would have been too little, had there not been something else. . . .

There is a shrine for Emma's memory which is well known to all Americans—even, curiously enough, to those who have never heard her name. In 1903, in an act "of loving memory," an admirer of Emma's, Georgiana Schuyler, arranged for her verses about the "huddled masses" to be engraved upon the pedestal of the Statue of Liberty. Since then a kind of kinship has existed between the Goddess of Liberty and Emma Lazarus' memory.

The Statue towers 305 feet above the sea, surpassing the legendary height of the Colossus of Rhodes. But the "halo" surrounding it must really be much greater than the actual light of its torch. What, otherwise, accounts for its being a beacon to the yearning masses in Europe, Africa and Asia, to the "tired," the "poor," the "huddled," and the "tempest-tost"?

Around Bedloe Island the winds sing, the waves slap, the sea gulls screech. Since 1886 millions of immigrants have passed by the goddess with the torch. And since 1903 many hundreds of thousands of visitors have read the name of Emma Lazarus. Most of them have forgotten it again. On July 22, 1949, the hundredth anniversary of the poet's birth, the name will be recalled and be seen and heard by many people for the first time. But what, after all, is a name? Names molder in libraries or wither in anthologies. Emma's name will not vanish so long as Liberty's statue stands; it is indissolubly joined with the mighty colossus on which her verses are graven.

SOURCES AND ACKNOWLEDGMENTS

INDEX

SOURCES AND ACKNOWLEDGMENTS

EVER SINCE 1920, when the *Cambridge History of American Literature* rescued Emma Lazarus from oblivion to place her beside Margaret Fuller, Julia Ward Howe and other eminent women in American letters, a new edition of her works could have been expected. But this had to wait until 1944, after the expiration of the copyright, when Morris U. Schappes brought out his *Emma Lazarus, Selections from Her Poetry and Prose* (New York), unhampered by Annie Lazarus' interdiction on the printing of anything with a Jewish theme. Schappes' selection could hardly be better; unfortunately it is much too small and is no substitute for what is still wanting today, an edition of Emma Lazarus' complete works.

Shortly before this there appeared two works which cast much light on the intellectual life of the poetess: *Letters to Emma Lazarus in the Columbia University Library* (New York 1939), edited by Ralph Lesley Rusk, among which there were Emerson's letters to Emma Lazarus (the letters Emma wrote to Emerson, in the possession of the Ralph Waldo Emerson Memorial Association, are still unpublished); and Richard H. A. Gottheil's *The Life of Gustav Gottheil, Memoir of a Priest in Israel* (Williamsport 1936), which dispelled once for all the legend that Emma Lazarus had evinced serious interest in Jewish affairs before the Russian pogroms of 1881. A collection of her letters—which we unfortunately do not as yet possess—would show how intense this interest was, lasting her whole life through, once it had been aroused. "It is desirable that a collection be published of all existent Lazarus letters, including those she addressed to and received from her eminent Jewish contemporaries," wrote Dr. Joshua Bloch in 1939 in the *Journal of Jewish Bibliography*.

Up to the time that the two aforementioned works appeared, the meager literature on Emma Lazarus was restricted to two sources: Josephine Lazarus' essay, often cited in these pages, in *The Century Magazine* in 1888; and the short biographical sketch by Henrietta Szold in *The Jewish Encyclopedia*, which culminated in these words: "Doubtless she is the most distinguished literary figure produced by American Jewry, and possibly the most eminent poet among Jews since Heine and Judah Löb Gordon."

The earliest mention made of Emma Lazarus in an American book was by Henry Samuel Morais, in his *Eminent Israelites of the Nineteenth Century* (Philadelphia 1880); he knows of the occasional poem on the Reverend I. I. Lyons, and of the translations of Gabirol, Halevy and Ibn Ezra that Emma had reluctantly made. Two years later in Germany, M. Kayserling gave her eleven lines in his *Die Jüdischen Frauen in der Geschichte, Literatur und Kunst* (Leipzig 1879). In 1892 already, Nahida Rémy, in her book *Das Jüdische Weib* (Leipzig), makes no mention of Emma's *Dance to Death*; it is rather her patriotic poems that are spoken of, among which the poem "Heroes" receives the greatest praise.

Thus, five years after the death of the poetess, awareness of the direction her spiritual development took has vanished. From time to time essays appeared that were able to appraise this development correctly, as for instance Mary M. Cohen's "Emma Lazarus: Woman, Poet, Patriot" (*Poet-lore*, Boston 1893); Rachel Cohen's "Emma Lazarus" (*Reform Advocate*, Chicago 1927); and W. I. Price's "Three Forgotten Poetesses" (*The Forum*, New York 1912). Sporadic mention was made of Emma Lazarus in the *Letters of Richard W. Gilder*, edited by his daughter Rosamond Gilder (Boston 1916), and in Constance Burton Harrison's *Recollections Grave and Gay* (New York 1911).

It is only in the last decade that Emma Lazarus has been made a subject of doctoral dissertations, doubtless because of the approaching centenary of her birth. In 1939 Geraldine Rosenfeld wrote her thesis for Columbia University on *Emma Lazarus and Heinrich Heine*. In 1942 this was followed by Sister Mary Joseph's thesis for Saint John's College, Brooklyn, entitled *Emma Lazarus*. Before this Judith Berlin-Liebermann had published a doctoral dissertation for the Hebrew University at Jerusalem on *Robert Browning and Hebraism*, and Arthur Zeiger is presently at work on a thesis on Emma Lazarus for New York University.

Important philological work was done by Max I. Baym in his *A Neglected Translator of Italian Poetry: Emma Lazarus* (*Italica*, Vol. XXI, 1945), who in addition contributed several essays to the *Publications of the American Jewish Society* ("Emma Lazarus' Indebtedness to George Eliot" and "Emma Lazarus' Approach to Renan"). Other special studies were made by Alfred Werner: "An American Deborah" (*Contemporary Jewish Record*, 1945), by Murray Frank: "Emma Lazarus—Symbol of Liberty" (*Chicago Jewish Forum*, 1948), and by Albert Mordell: "The 100th Birthday of Emma Lazarus," a comprehensive essay written for the *Jewish Book Annual* (1948–49). In increasing measure pages or even chapters have been allotted to her in various books: Philip Cowen's *Memories of an American Jew* (Philadelphia 1932), Allan Lesser's *Weave a Wreath of Laurel* (New York 1939), Van Wyck Brooks' *The Times of Melville and Whitman* (New York 1947), Solomon Grayzel's *A History of the Jews* (Philadelphia 1947), Theodore Maynard's *A Fire Was Lighted*, and Hertha Pauli's and E. B. Ashton's account of the Statue of Liberty, *I Lift My Lamp* (New York 1948).

The author of this book is indebted to all these writers for the assistance their works afforded him. In treating of the chief enigma in the life of Emma Lazarus—her strong attachment to her father, which would seem to have precluded her marrying—the author was able to draw on certain English sources. It was to her English friends that Emma spoke of her youth, chiefly to William Morris. Morris passed this knowledge on to his friends Edward Carpenter (1844–1929), the social reformer, who had made Emma's personal acquaintance around 1885, and William Parnes, who had met her as far back as 1883 in London. Interest in Emma Lazarus has been alive in England since; and when M. A. Spielmann delivered her Lazarus lecture in 1918 before the West End Society in London, she was approached by Parnes who had in mind the foundation of an Emma Lazarus society. The project came to nought when Parnes had to leave for the Continent.

The author wishes to thank all those persons and institutions that greatly facilitated his research: Dr. Alexander Marx of the Jewish Theological Seminary of New York; Rabbi Isidore Meyer of the American Historical Jewish Society; Dr. Joshua Bloch of the Jewish Division of the New York Public Library; Rabbi David de Sola Pool of the Congregation Shearith Israel; the British Museum; Edward O'Brien and William Parnes of London, for very valuable information about Emma Lazarus' early life; and Mrs. Frances Nathan Wolff of New York, cousin of Emma Lazarus.

INDEX

A

Adams, Henry: 135
Aldrich, Thomas Bailey: 162
Alexander II: 81-83, 87, 88, 102, 105, 107
Alexander III: 82, 83, 88, 154
Asch, Sholom: 161
Austen, Jane: 17, 56

B

Bartholdi, Auguste: 177
Battersea, Lady: 166
Baym, Max I.: 182-83, 201, 217
Belinski, Andrei: 118-19
Bernhardt, Sarah: 137
Brafman, Jacob: 114
Brandes, Georg M. C.: 109-10, 208
Brion, Friederike: 56, 59
Brooks, Van Wyck: 63, 197, 217
Browning, Elizabeth Barrett: 166, 168-69, 171, 189
Browning, Robert: 49, 68, 164-72, 177, 181, 188, 193, 204
Bryant, William Cullen: 51
Burns, Robert: 51, 131
Byron, Lord: 24, 30, 48, 51, 64-68, 79, 91, 97, 142, 170, 173, 186

C

Carpenter, Edward: 218
Cather, Willa: 135-36
Channing, William Ellery: 62-64
Chaucer: 43, 51
Chopin, Frederic: 26, 134
Clemenceau, Georges: 208
Cleveland, Grover: 190
Cowen, Philip: 119-20, 132-33, 146-47, 167, 205, 208, 217

D

Dana, Charles A.: 72, 133
Dante: 161, 182, 184
Delacroix, Eugène: 181
Dickinson, Emily: 135
Disraeli, Benjamin: 83, 103, 109-12
Donizetti: 70
Dostoevsky: 33
Dreyfus, Alfred: 206
Dreyfus, Lucie: 207
Duse, Eleanora: 113

E

Eliot, George: 28, 119-24, 137-39, 155, 164, 183

219

Emerson, Ellen: 45, 48, 61
Emerson, Lidian: 45, 61, 199
Emerson, Ralph Waldo: 30-41, 45, 48-57, 60-64, 67-69, 79, 101, 130, 154, 162, 165, 182, 196, 215
Euripides: 39, 49
Evans, Marian: *see* Eliot, George
Evarts, William M.: 104-106, 119, 136, 178
Ezra, Ibn: 80

F

Falk, Bernard: 142
Feuerbach, Ludwig: 138
Flaubert, Gustave: 34
Frederic, Harold: 84-85
Frothingham, N. L: 51
Fuller, Margaret: 182

G

Gabirol, Ibn: 80, 154
Garfield, James: 181
George, Henry: 161, 180, 188
Gilder, Helena de Kay: 112-13, 140, 145
Gilder, Richard Watson: 112-13, 115-16, 140, 145, 199, 211, 216
Goethe: 33, 43, 45, 56, 58-60, 80, 138, 163, 185, 192
Goldsmid, Sir Julian: 166
Gosse, Sir Edmund: 165
Gottheil, Gustav: 75-81, 110, 118, 124, 144, 164, 203, 215
Gottheil, Richard H. A.: 80, 215
Grant, Ulysses S.: 24, 104, 106
Greeley, Horace: 16

H

Halevi, Jehuda Ben: 80, 154
Hamilton, Lady Emma: 18

Hardy, Thomas, 166
Harrison, Constance: 188, 199, 211, 216
Harte, Bret: 51, 178
Hawthorne, Nathaniel: 145, 182
Hawthorne, Rose: 145, 162, 168-69, 205-6
Hay, John: 136
Heine, Heinrich: 26, 29, 30, 80, 92, 101, 134-35, 161, 170, 182, 190, 200-1
Heilprin, Michael: 127, 128, 129, 164
Higginson, Thomas Wentworth: 27, 58, 183
Howe, Julia Ward: 51, 215
Howells, William Dean: 49, 50, 56, 174
Hugo, Victor: 29, 30, 80, 161
Huxley, Henrietta: 165

I

Irving, Washington: 130

J

Jackson, Andrew: 14
James, Henry: 57, 168, 180
James, William: 67, 179
Johnstone, Annie Humphreys: *see* Lazarus, Annie

K

Kay, Charles De: 55
Keats, John: 186
Kipling, Rudyard: 113

L

Laboulaye, Edouard de: 177
Lazarus, Agnes: 14, 28, 72
Lazarus, Annie: 14, 72, 133, 162, 165, 207-10

Lazarus, Eliezer Frank: 15, 38
Lazarus, Hettie: 15, 18, 23, 27, 50, 61
Lazarus, Jack: 71
Lazarus, Josephine: 14, 17, 18, 20, 62, 68, 71, 72, 141, 164, 180, 185-86, 199-200, 206-8, 211, 216
Lazarus, Mary: 14, 72
Lazarus, Moses: 14-16, 18-20, 27, 28, 35, 38, 71, 72, 85, 133-34, 180, 208
Lazarus, Sarah: 14, 72, 200
Lessing: 101
Lewisohn, Ludwig: 135
Lewes, George Henry: 138-39
Lincoln, Abraham: 21, 24, 25, 26, 76, 87, 105, 125, 197
Longfellow, Henry Wadsworth: 130-32, 165, 178, 182
Lowell, James Russell: 48, 49, 179-80, 182, 199
Lyons, Jacques: 79, 216

M

Mann, Thomas: 190
Maynard, Theodore: 112, 217
Mendelssohn, Moses: 56, 101
Menken, Adah Isaacs: 139-42
Mill, John Stuart: 122
Milton: 22, 23
Mordell, Albert: 199, 217
Morris, William: 39, 50, 174-77, 181, 184, 218
Musset, Alfred de: 80, 134, 161, 172

N

Napoleon: 101, 103
Nathan, Benjamin: 50
Nathan, Hettie: *see* Lazarus, Hettie

Nathan, Isaac: 91
Nathan, Seixas: 50
Nekrasov: 88
Nietzsche: 68

O

Oliphant, Laurence: 136-37, 164

P

Paderewski, Jan: 113
Parnes, William B.: 177, 187, 188, 211, 218
Partridge, E. L.: 205
Perovskaya, Sophi: 88
Petrarch: 161, 182, 183
Pfefferkorn, Johannes: 114
Philippson, Martin: 166
Plato: 33
Poe, Edgar Allan: 55, 180-81
Procter, Anne Skepper: 168

R

Ragozin, Zinaida Alexeievna: 113-19
Rashi: 154
Rembrandt: 86, 182, 189
Repplier, Agnes: 199
Reuchlin, Johannes: 114
Richards, Bernard G.: 208-10
Rosenthal, Herman: 126-27
Rossetti, Dante Gabriel: 161, 175
Rothschild, Baron Nathaniel: 141, 166
Rusk, Ralph L.: 45, 61, 69, 215

S

Salvini, Tommaso: 145-46, 184
Sand, George: 28, 134
Santa-Maria, Solomon Levi-Paul de: 96-97

221

Schappes, Morris U.: 215
Schiller: 29, 101, 152
Schnabel, Louis: 144, 160
Schumann, Robert: 26, 180, 190-91
Schuyler, Georgiana: 212
Scott, Walter: 17
Seixas, Gershom: 209
Shakespeare: 23, 40, 51, 59, 155, 173, 187
Shelley: 170, 186-87
Simon, Sir John: 166-67
Spencer, Herbert: 133, 138
Spinoza: 117, 154
Stedman, Edmund Clarence: 94, 161, 204, 211
Stowe, Harriet Beecher: 204
Suvorin, Boris: 115

T

Taine, Hippolyte: 163
Taylor, Bayard: 131
Tennyson, Lord Alfred: 50
Thoreau: 37, 62, 63, 64
Tolstoy: 33

Traubel, Horace: 199
Turgeniev, Ivan: 57, 58, 59, 60
Twain, Mark: 178

V

Victoria, Queen: 105, 109, 141
Vives, Joshua Ibn: 96, 97

W

Wagner, Richard: 41, 147
Ward, Samuel G.: 30, 33, 72
Washington, George: 20, 125
Whitman, Walt: 53, 113, 130, 145, 178, 196-99, 211
Whittier, John Greenleaf: 170, 204
Wilson, Edmund: 196
Wolff, Frances Nathan: 218

Z

Zeiger, Arthur: 217
Zola, Emile: 207
Zweig, Stefan: 208

CPSIA information can be obtained
at www.ICGtesting.com
Printed in the USA
LVHW022115270219
608942LV00019B/1253